house

DESIGN WITH ARCHITECTS

RIBA Publishing

RUTH SLAVID

© RIBA Publishing, 2022

Published by RIBA Publishing, 66 Portland Place, London, W1B 1AD

ISBN 9781914124501

The right of Ruth Slavid to be identified as the Author of this Work has been asserted in accordance with the Copyright, Designs and Patents Act 1988 sections 77 and 78.

British Library Cataloguing-in-Publication Data

A catalogue record for this book is available from the British Library.

Commissioning Editor: Clare Holloway

Assistant Editor: Scarlet Furness

Production: Jane Rogers

Designed and typeset by Studio Kalinka

Printed and bound by Short Run Press, Exeter

Cover image: Sycamore Hall, Paul Testa Architecture, photography by Dug Wilders

While every effort has been made to check the accuracy and quality of the information given in this publication, neither the Author nor the Publisher accept any responsibility for the subsequent use of this information, for any errors or omissions that it may contain, or for any misunderstandings arising from it.

www.ribapublishing.com

acknowledgements

I have been writing about architecture for a long time, and about the construction industry for even longer. Almost everybody I have met, whether colleague, architect, or another construction professional, has contributed to my knowledge and hence to my ability to write this book. So, all deserve my thanks.

More particular thanks must go to the architects who agreed to have their projects included, to the clients who provided insight, and to the photographers who showed them off so well.

I also want to thank Clare Holloway at the RIBA who came up with the original idea for this book and encouraged me throughout, Scarlet Furness who chased image permissions tirelessly, and Jane Rogers for her production work.

Finally, I want to thank Jeffrey Borinsky, who became my husband while I was writing this book and who has provided unfailing support and encouragement.

foreword

We are quick to judge. And we are quite good at it too. We think of ourselves as arbiters of taste and design, connoisseurs of architecture, schooled by countless television series (partly my fault here) and legion design magazines. Daily, we walk through urban spaces, public buildings and homes. We decorate, plan loft extensions and order garden pods. We all appear highly competent when it comes to building and that's partly because so many of us have become space creators ourselves. We all, it seems, are architects.

Yet we fall so far short of what architects can achieve for us. You and I may be able to rip out some pictures from magazines and catalogues but we cannot begin to manipulate materials, space and light (as well as conduits, concrete and building regulations) into breathtaking experiences that embody not just our dreams but our hopes and values; experiences which have the power to even improve who we are. The right architect can do that, as can be seen in the exemplary projects in this volume. They can deliver you your future.

If you have ever tried to paint a picture or lay out a garden or design a bathroom you will be cognisant of the paralysing fear of choice, of what Will Self has called 'the infinite potentiality of outcomes'. If anything is possible, at every turn the thread of your work can take a turn towards the sublime or, in an instant, the dreadful. Or just simply the mundane.

If you have ever enjoyed the good fortune of working with an architect who sees the world as you do then you will know how, like a great author or chef, they are able to take your vision and brief and not just make it real but interpret it into something bigger and altogether more vivid and fully resolved in all its details. You might have a shopping list of ingredients; you might even have bought the spoon; they will, in return, create the most perfect syllabub.

And, if you choose this path – as an amateur space creator, as a collaborator with an architect – you too potentially bring something transformative to the relationship. Because working with an architect does not make you a customer, nor necessarily even a client. It gives you the chance to become a patron.

Transforming a house to suit your needs is always challenging and often stressful but in the right circumstances, with a talented professional alongside, it can be empowering, ennobling and joyful too. This volume is both a guide and inspiration for that journey.

Kevin McCloud

contents

introduction

You are probably reading this because you are at least thinking about making some changes to your home. This is a daunting, exciting task and a serious financial commitment.

There is so much to think about. Should you improve your home or should you move instead? Do you want to realise your dreams or are you just going to do the minimum that you can get away with or afford? You probably know what is wrong with your house, but do you really know what would make it better?

The aim of this book is to help in this process and, in particular, to convince you that the result of your efforts is likely to be far more successful if you work with an architect. Perhaps you should think of your relationship with an architect as similar to dealing with a doctor. You know what is troubling you, what your symptoms are. But then you speak to the professional who can, you hope, diagnose your underlying problem and suggest a treatment.

That, however, is where the analogy breaks down. A good doctor should provide an accurate diagnosis for which there is probably one recommended treatment. If you get a second opinion, it is most likely that you will end up with the same diagnosis and treatment. But every architect will approach a problem in a different way, interpret your request differently and propose a different solution. There may be similarities in approach just as there are in buildings, but your choice of architect is crucial. This is both scary and part of the pleasure of finding and working with a good architect.

The book is divided into two parts. The first is a collection of projects designed by architects, varying in scale from those that cost around £40,000 to others at more than half a million pounds (costs given at the start of each case study are approximate). I have separated the case studies in Part 1 into five categories for convenience, looking at the desire for more space, at homes with new basements, at unusual problems and places, at homes where sustainability is top of the agenda, and at projects where there is a great desire for an improved connection with a garden or the wider outdoor world. Obviously there is an overlap. For example, if you want more space, it may be that building a basement is the right solution for you. And all projects, whatever the primary motivation, should include improved environmental credentials.

There are city-centre flats, a Georgian townhouse, a bungalow with magnificent views of countryside, an old schoolhouse and even a wrecked building that has been restored to still look like a wreck. Nobody will like all these projects because some will not accord with their personal taste, but they all have merits. The point of including them is that, as well as providing visual pleasure, they show what a talented architect can do.

The second part of this book is less about inspiration and more about understanding. It explains what architects do and looks at the ways that clients can choose them, brief them and work with them. It aims to demystify the process and to address some common fears and concerns. It shows that, although the decisions involved in deciding to improve your home are important ones, you should not be afraid. I hope you enjoy this book and go on to gain pleasure from a greatly improved home.

◄

0.1 WORK(OUT) FROM HOME BY SCENARIO ARCHITECTURE, SEE PAGE 36.

making
more space

1

anting more space is probably the primary reason for moving or reconfiguring a property. Moving is expensive. In London, for example, in November 2021, the median price for a one-bedroom property was £400,000. For two bedrooms it was £575,000; for three bedrooms £775,000 and for four bedrooms £1,050,000.[1] In other words, all things being equal, the cost of moving somewhere with an extra bedroom was around £200,000. And all things are usually not equal. You may not be able to move in the area where you are currently living and where, crucially, your children are at school. You may have to give up a garden on which you have worked, or a space that suits your particular needs. You will certainly incur additional costs. Stamp duty is a graduated tax, with rates rising from zero for the cheapest properties to 10% on the most expensive. In England and Northern Ireland, at the time of writing, the stamp duty for a property costing £700,000 is £25,000, according to the government's stamp duty calculator.[2] There are also, of course, removal costs.

And once you buy your new property, there will probably be more that you want to do. Whether it needs serious work, or a new kitchen, or just a change of flooring, it is unlikely to be cost-free. Why not, then, stay where you are and create the home you want from the one you already love?

This is not a new idea. The London discussion and exhibition forum New London Architecture has been running an annual competition entitled 'Don't move, improve!' for more than 10 years, celebrating the best-designed improvements. And there is no shortage. The variety is huge, and you can see some of that variety in this book. Extensions can go upwards or in any of four directions, or be stand-alone projects in a garden. They can also go downwards, although that is the subject of a separate chapter. And they can, and should, respond to the particular needs of households.

The largest driver for enlarging a home is an increase in the size of a household – whether through a new relationship, the birth of children or an older relative moving in. In addition, the need for a place to work has become a particular concern. There have always been people who worked from home and needed a space in which to do it – look at George Bernard Shaw's enchanting rotating writing hut at Ayot St Lawrence, Hertfordshire – but the Covid-19 pandemic has thrown this into sharp perspective.

People started working at home with no notice, and in many cases the accommodation they had proved woefully inadequate. Yet there is an appetite for working from home that is resulting in many people travelling to workplaces for only some of their working days. Again, ingenuity is needed to make that room within what may be a limited curtilage, within planning constraints and within the limits of a budget.

The projects in this chapter are excellent examples of what can be done. Some comprise a relatively standard solution, but one completed with sensitivity and spatial intelligence. Others are near miraculous – the homes that are extended out into unpromising scraps of land, or the house that gains an extra floor when it seems that that is impossible.

1.1 TWO-AND-A-HALF -STOREY HOUSE BY BRADLEY VAN DER STRAETEN ARCHITECTS, SEE PAGE 4.

Two-and-a-Half-Storey House

ARCHITECT: BRADLEY VAN DER STRAETEN ARCHITECTS

LOCATION: LONDON

BUDGET: £110,000

PROJECT FINISHED: 2020

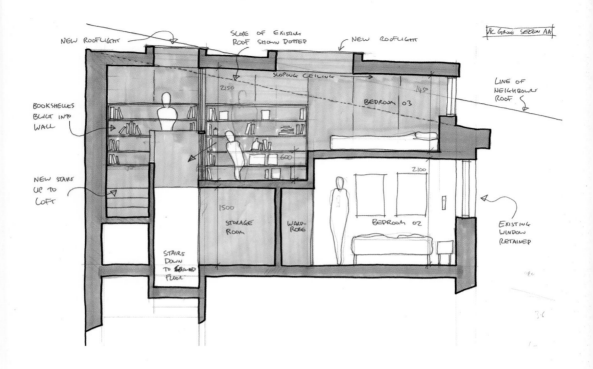

Labels on sketch: NEW ROOFLIGHT — SLOPE OF EXISTING ROOF SHOWN DOTTED — NEW ROOFLIGHT — VIC GRINE SECTION AA — SLOPING CEILING — LINE OF NEIGHBOURS ROOF — 2150 — BEDROOM 03 — 1450 — BOOKSHELVES BUILT INTO WALL — 600 — NEW STAIRS UP TO LOFT — 2100 — 1500 — STORAGE ROOM — WARDROBE — BEDROOM 02 — STAIRS DOWN TO GROUND FLOOR — EXISTING WINDOW RETAINED

1.3 ARCHITECT'S SKETCH
SHOWING THE CLEVER
GEOMETRY

1.2 THE INGENIOUS
DESIGN FITS WITHIN
THE PLANNERS'
STRINGENT HEIGHT
REQUIREMENTS

At this house on a central London housing estate, Bradley Van Der Straeten Architects have solved a seemingly impossible problem. They have created an extra room in the roof of a building where planning restrictions dictated that there was no room to do so. Hence the name 'Two-and-a-Half-Storey House'.

The design, with all its ingenuity, was driven by necessity. The couple who owned the house, which had only two bedrooms, were expecting a second child. They needed another bedroom, but couldn't afford to move to a three-bedroom property in the area. So they decided to look at expansion. The problem was that their roof had a lower profile than its neighbours and the planners felt that this distinction should be preserved, turning down two planning applications for a single-storey upward extension.

5

What Bradley Van Der Straeten Architects came up with has a 'half height' roof extension, one that made it possible to create an extra room within the height limits imposed by the planners. They did this by slotting the extra room above an existing one, stepping up to a bed platform in an area that was only half-height. The half-height space was above a full-height room; the full-height area was above service spaces such as the boiler room that didn't themselves need to be at full height. In effect, there are two vertical L-shapes that slot together, allowing this clever bit of geometric gymnastics. The name of the project is, as the architects have said, reminiscent of the existence of a seventh-and-a-half floor in the film *Being John Malkovich* but the effect is not.

We have all seen houses that have been converted or extended to fit more people in, with a result that is poky or awkward. This is quite the opposite. Everything feels finished and considered, with the use of light-coloured plywood throughout making the space feel bright, modern and, yes, generous. And all this for £110,000, which was less than the cost of moving to a bigger property.

The architects explained, 'We approached the design as an interlocking jigsaw. We knew the half-height of the loft was fixed so the design was all about creating two interlocking floor levels in the space of one and a half floors. We may have given less footprint, but we created more volume and an additional bedroom by using it creatively.'

Roof windows ensure that the bedroom is light, and the integration of the bedframe within the design allows space for circulation. The plywood not only knits the old and new areas together but also conceals a lot of clever storage spaces.

In order to get as much headroom as possible, the architect had to detail everything to the millimetre. Some of the structural timbers in the ceilings are exposed. Insulation is with vacuum insulation panels – not the cheapest option, but the one that takes up the least space.

The clients said, 'It's a really easy family house to live in and we love being able to see our eldest son playing in his room using the hallway window. From the moment my son saw his room he loved it and will play for hours in there! Considering the limited amount of "actual" floor space we have added, the feeling of space is incredible, and the amount of storage sets this project apart.'

They added, 'If you have conviction in the initial idea, make sure you follow it through fully. At some points, we started to have doubts about the spaces we were creating but now that it is finished, we are blown away with the design and we couldn't be happier.'

They recognised the value of working with an architect, saying, 'Working with an architect who has really thought about the detail is important. George [Bradley] and the team at BVDS created a house that we can truly live in. Every corner of the house has been considered and thought through to make living easier.'

▲
1.4 THE BED PLATFORM FORMS
THE CEILING OF THE ROOM
BELOW. SHELVING IS CREATED
FROM THE TIMBER INTERIOR

**Bradley Van Der Straeten
Architects have solved
a seemingly impossible
problem.**

◄
1.5 STAIRCASE LEADING
UP TO THE NEW ROOM

Room for an Opera Singer

ARCHITECT: FAB ARCHITECTS

LOCATION: LONDON

BUDGET: £40,000

PROJECT FINISHED: 2020

We all learnt during the Covid-19 pandemic how important it can be to put some distance between our homes and work. For those who have a garden, one answer may be to build a special space in it. There are lots of off-the-shelf options available, but anybody who has specific needs will get a great benefit from having something designed just for them.

This is what Alex and Jo, a couple in west London, did, calling on FAB Architects, who they already knew. In addition to having their own specific requirements, they also needed to satisfy the planners, as this is a conservation area. The result is a 3m by 4m space, with arched entrances and a circular rooflight that is pleasing to look at and fulfils the clients' needs. Alex is an opera singer who needed somewhere to practise without waking their new baby. Jo wanted a quiet space away from the house where she could work remotely – presumably not at the same time! At other times, the pair use the space for entertaining.

Like many projects, this one evolved during the design process. Originally the façade was to be ceramic but in the final design it is of Kebony, a softwood that has been treated with natural chemicals to make it more durable and behave more like a hardwood.

The building sits above the roots of a tree. The architect consulted an arboriculturist and, as a result, the building has special screw foundations that avoid the roots.

The actual structure is relatively simple, consisting of structural insulated panels (SIPs), although the arches made it a little more complicated. It was, however, within the range of a small contractor. In fact, for FAB, this was the first building in a collaboration with a company called Luna Spaces, which makes architect-designed garden rooms.

The architects said, 'We have found our best projects come from clear briefs and creative solutions to the challenges in that brief. Some guidance for clients would be to take the time to consider what it is you are looking to get out of the space in the short, medium and long term. For garden rooms in particular, it can be a daunting process leafing through the multitude of websites offering similar things. Our advice here is to seek out a designer who matches with your design ambitions and work with them to create something designed around your family's needs.'

1.6 THE NEW ROOM IS A WELCOMING ADDITION TO THE GARDEN

1.7 IN GOOD WEATHER, THE ROOM CAN OPEN UP TO THE GARDEN

1.8 A ROOFLIGHT
MAKES THE SPACE
BRIGHTER

'Our best projects come from clear briefs and creative solutions to the challenges in that brief.'

1.9 LOOKING BACK
TOWARDS
THE HOUSE

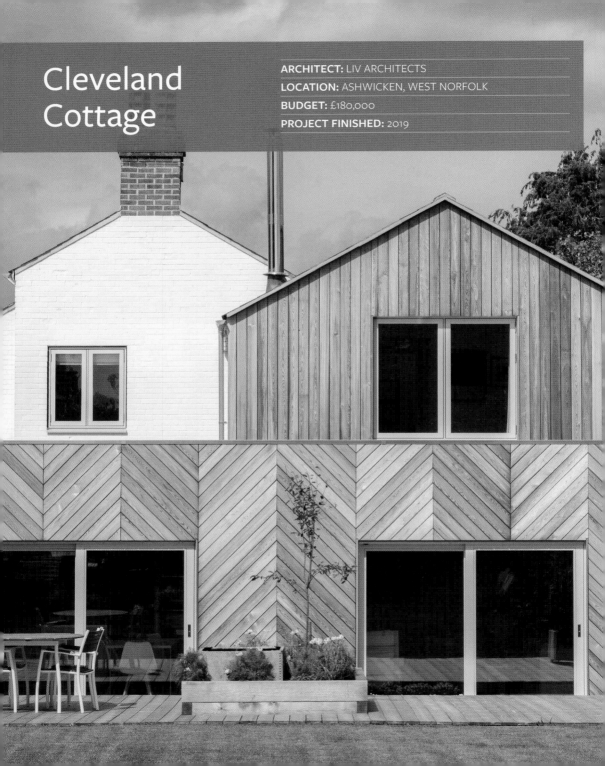

Cleveland Cottage

ARCHITECT: LIV ARCHITECTS

LOCATION: ASHWICKEN, WEST NORFOLK

BUDGET: £180,000

PROJECT FINISHED: 2019

◄
1.10 THE NEW
EXTENSION WRAPS
AROUND THE
ORIGINAL COTTAGE
BUT ONLY TOUCHES
IT AT THREE POINTS
– ESSENTIAL FOR
THE PROGRAMME,
WITH THE OWNERS
REMAINING
IN RESIDENCE
THROUGHOUT
CONSTRUCTION.

Not only was this two-up, two-down cottage too small for its new owners, it also ignored its substantial garden, turning a blank face towards it. This setup was due to the fact that the building had originally been an annexe to the house next door, and was angled to turn its back on that house. It had a couple of unsympathetic extensions, which were removed as part of the improvement works.

The previous owner had legally separated the two houses with the Land Registry but without obtaining planning approval. As a result, during planning for these works, the client had to pay the Community Infrastructure Levy due on new developments. Otherwise, planning went smoothly.

The clients' brief, while not unusual, was demanding. They wanted more space than the existing 1930s building offered; they had a relatively limited budget; and they wanted to remain in the building while the works were taking place. This is a major constraint. Obviously, if somebody moves

▲
1.11 IN ADDITION TO BEING TOO SMALL, THE 'ORIGINAL' BUILDING HAD UNSYMPATHETIC EXTENSIONS AND TURNED ITS BACK ON THE GARDEN.

▼
1.12 DRAWING SHOWING, FROM LEFT TO RIGHT: THE HOUSE AS BOUGHT BY THE CURRENT OWNERS; THE HOUSE WITH THE UNSYMPATHETIC EXTENSIONS REMOVED; THE FINISHED BUILDING.

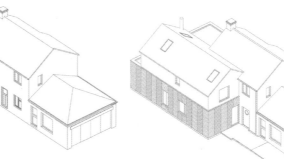

◄

1.13 THE TIMBER-
CLAD EXTENSIONS
SIT COMFORTABLY
WITH THE ORIGINAL
COTTAGE.

The extension, which is clad in timber, in contrast to the brick of the original structure, has much improved thermal properties.

▶

1.14 THE LIGHT-
FILLED KITCHEN.

out of their house while building works are going on, they have to pay to stay somewhere else. But, where work affects the entire building, it is both faster and easier if the builders have the run of the place.

The owners' determination to stay in place affected the design. The new element is an L-shape, and it only touches the existing building at three points. This meant that during the first part of the work, the owners could remain in the cottage while the new work went on. Then they moved into the new extension while work was done on the original building, and finally the two were joined together at the three points.

The wraparound extension to the side and rear adds a broken-plan kitchen/dining/living space plus two further bedrooms and a new staircase. The main living spaces now look out over the rear south-facing gardens, and the new staircase means that space can be used more effectively within the existing cottage.

The extension, which is clad in timber, in contrast to the brick of the original structure, has much improved thermal properties. These have also been increased as far as possible in the existing building, with insulated plasterboard linings and loft insulation, plus new windows. An air-source heat pump replaces the oil-fired boiler. As a result of all this, the Energy Performance Certificate (EPC) of the building has risen from F to D.

Although the clients employed a main contractor to construct the shell of the building as far as making it watertight, they then managed all the internal trades themselves, including actually doing finishing work such as fitting kitchens, tiling and decorating. This saved more money, and was probably the only advantage of going through the uncomfortable experience of living on site throughout the works.

And the end result? Definitely worth the pain.

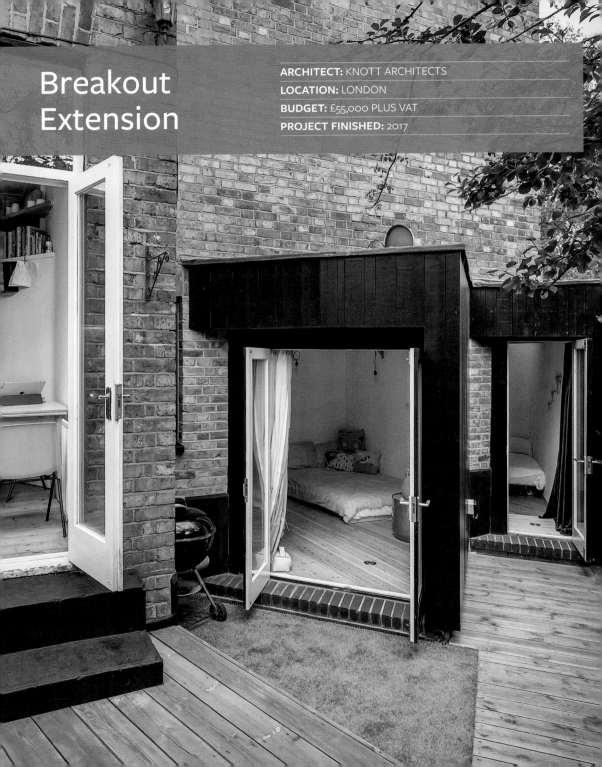

Breakout
Extension

ARCHITECT: KNOTT ARCHITECTS
LOCATION: LONDON
BUDGET: £55,000 PLUS VAT
PROJECT FINISHED: 2017

◀
1.15 THE TWO
EXTENSIONS JUT
OUT INTO THE
AWKWARD-SHAPED
GARDEN.

▼
1.16 THE PLAN
SHOWS THE NEW
ARRANGEMENT,
WITH AN
ADDITIONAL
BEDROOM AND
THE ORIGINAL
BEDROOM AND
THE BATHROOM
RECONFIGURED.

This extension, in Crouch End, north London, solves a typical problem, but in an atypical way. A couple living in a small one-bedroom flat had a baby and needed an extra room. They chose Knott Architects not only because they liked the work on the website but also because the practice had connections in the area.

The obvious move was to expand into the garden but this was not as easy as in many properties, because there was only a small rear-side garden, with skewed boundary fences, leaving only minimal space at an awkward angle.

The most economical solution, the architect advised, was to create two extensions, one breaking out from the existing bedroom. This was effectively brought forward, allowing access to the new second bedroom, in what had previously been an unregarded corner of the garden.

In that corner, the roof is, as the architect put it, 'prised open' – instead of being horizontal, the base of the roof lifts up at an angle and small triangular windows are inserted in the gaps to bring in more light. Insulation levels have been improved in both the new and, where possible, the existing parts of the flat. The new bedroom, in particular, has an intriguing form, with

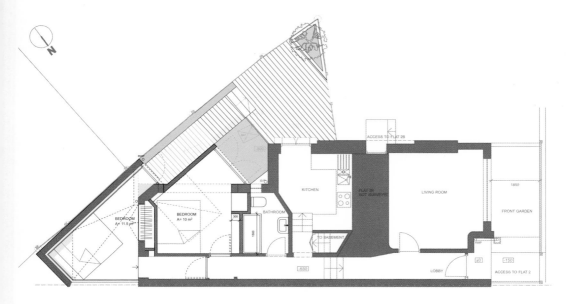

the rafters running across at an angle and the bricks of what was previously an external wall left exposed.

The project is in a conservation area, which could cause problems with an innovative idea. But the architect worked hard to make the planning process as smooth as possible, seeking pre-application advice from the planning department and also consulting neighbours.

The project went out to tender to three contractors, and was won by a small firm that had been recommended to the client. Knott Architects had not previously worked with this contractor, so there was an initial

process of getting to know each other, and understanding how each other worked. The architect said, 'This required a little more site supervision than normal, but the results were good.' They added, 'On small jobs like this it is important to have a very good relationship with the clients, and to understand the essence of their needs, and to explore the detail with them.'

When the project completed in 2017, the clients had gained an extra bedroom and an improved flat for the modest sum of £55,000 plus VAT – far less than the cost of moving to a larger property.

1.17 THE NEW BEDROOM AND CORRIDOR. THE BRICKS OF WHAT WAS AN EXTERNAL WALL ARE EXPOSED.

1.19 A NEW BATHROOM FORMS PART OF THE PROJECT.

1.18 ADDITIONAL LIGHT COMES INTO THE NEW BEDROOM THROUGH WINDOWS BELOW THE 'PRISED OPEN' ROOF.

This extension, in Crouch End, north London, solves a typical problem, but in an atypical way.

Lambeth Marsh House

ARCHITECT: FRAHER ARCHITECTS

LOCATION: LONDON

BUDGET: CONFIDENTIAL

PROJECT FINISHED: 2015

1.20 THE GLAZED
EXTENSION HAS AN
UNUSUAL GEOMETRY.

Look at the rear extension of this house
in Lambeth, south London, and it will
immediately strike you as different from
most side returns. Obviously every project
has its own character, but the difference
here is greater. There is something about
the geometry that is surprising. The clue is
at the front of the house.

Lambeth Marsh House sits in a brick
terrace of modest houses originally
developed for artisan workers. Now part of
a conservation area, the street is charming
in its consistency and its very ordinariness.
But look at the front doors and the roofs
and you will realise something odd.

**There is something about
the geometry that is
surprising. The clue is at
the front of the house.**

1.21 THE LIGHTS IN THE
HOUSE MAKE CLEAR
THE UNUSUAL POSITION
OF THE ROOF RIDGES
– AT THE SIDES OF THE
HOUSES RATHER THAN
THE CENTRE.

1.22 MUCH MORE LIGHT COMES INTO THE KITCHEN AND DINING AREA, WHICH IS ALSO CONSIDERABLY MORE SPACIOUS THAN PREVIOUSLY.

1.23 WORK THROUGHOUT
THE HOUSE IS TO A HIGH
STANDARD.

In most terraces, each house will have a roof ridge in the middle. But here, the gulley is in the middle, rising to a ridge at either side of the house. It is this unusual geometry that has influenced the design of the extension.

The house had been empty for 10 years before the client bought it and commissioned the architect to give it a new life. This included respecting the heritage and restoring some of the lost historic detailing. The architect restored the panelled fireplaces, wood panelling to the walls, architraves and skirting to their original condition, and then added the rear extension. Largely glazed, it both helps to create a spacious area for cooking and eating, and brings more light into the rear of the house.

Unusually for an architecture practice, Fraher have their own joinery company, Fraher & Co, which made and installed all the joinery. This is a level of control and quality that must have been of great benefit to the client.

◄

1.24 THE ARCHITECTURE PRACTICE HAVE THEIR OWN JOINERY COMPANY THAT UNDERTOOK ALL THE WOODWORK, INCLUDING RESTORING THE PANELLING.

Longhurst

ARCHITECT: GAGARIN STUDIO

LOCATION: MARPLE BRIDGE, GREATER MANCHESTER

BUDGET: £150,000

PROJECT FINISHED: 2013

Look at the back of this project on the edge of Marple Bridge in Greater Manchester and it will be clear to you that there is a rear extension. In fact, this extension is on two storeys, with the upper floor cleverly disguised to blend in with the original Victorian house. In contrast, the bright, light-coloured ground-floor extension is an evident and deliberate addition.

The reason the client wanted the work done was largely because the formal internal arrangement of the house no longer suited them, and they wanted a better connection to the garden. They appointed Gagarin, then a very young practice, who designed an extension that effectively infilled the L-shaped plan on the upper level to improve the arrangement of bedrooms and bathrooms on the first floor and attic.

At ground level, the extension pushes out further. The clearly modern addition gives new connections to the garden. Its white-rendered bay, which includes a window seat, frames key views from the house. Internally, the architect has opened up the rear of the ground floor. A change in level results in a light and modern kitchen/dining/garden area that sits level with the terrace outside it. A rooflight brings in additional light.

The client said, 'If we were ever in doubt about whether to engage the services of an architect in the redesign and extension of our family home, that was soon dispelled by the wonderful Gagarin Studio team. Several years on and we still admire the space created, and the detail realised, in a way that would never have been possible without their vision.'

◄
1.25 THIS VIEW FROM THE REAR SHOWS CLEARLY THE EXTRA SPACE THAT HAS BEEN ADDED AT GROUND LEVEL. THE FIRST-FLOOR EXTENSION BLENDS IN.

▲
1.26 THE HOUSE, BEFORE WORK BEGAN.

1.27 ROOFLIGHTS BRING
DAYLIGHT INTO THE
GENEROUS INTERIOR
SPACE.

▼

1.28 CONNECTION
TO THE GARDEN IS
GREATLY IMPROVED.

Paramount
Court

ARCHITECT: KNOX BHAVAN ARCHITECTS

LOCATION: LONDON

BUDGET: CONFIDENTIAL

PROJECT FINISHED: 2019

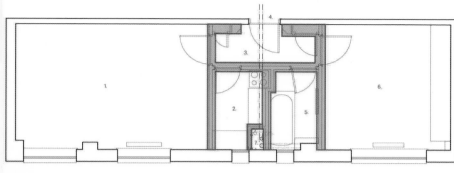

Demolish Existing Partition Walls

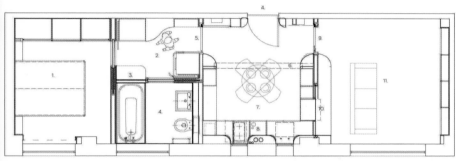

1.29 PLAN OF THE FLAT SHOWING THE WALLS THAT HAD TO BE DEMOLISHED AND, BELOW, THE NEW ARRANGEMENT.

1.30 VIEW FROM THE LIVING ROOM INTO THE KITCHEN. NOTE THE EXQUISITE JOINERY.

In many cases, creating extra space involves making an addition to a building, but in the case of the compact apartment that Knox Bhavan Architects transformed, this was not possible. Instead, by clever planning, attention to detail and a real understanding of what can and cannot be done, the architect created a feeling of spaciousness where there was none before.

The tiny flat is on the top floor of a 1930s block just off central London's Tottenham Court Road. Many of the flats are student accommodation and this was the purpose for which the clients originally bought it in the 1980s. Their daughter lived there while she was at university and then they took it over as their London pied-à-terre when they retired.

When they realised just how inconvenient the flat was, they sought an architect and were recommended to use Knox Bhavan, who found a way to provide more storage, more usable space and a rather 1930s nautical vibe that is in keeping with the Art Deco style of the building.

One of the problems was that the flat, as originally constituted, had a tiny kitchen and bathroom. The new design replaces them with a central kitchen that is big enough to eat in, a new bathroom in part of what was the sitting room, and a flip of the bedroom and sitting room, so that the sitting room can take advantage of the best window.

The architect created a feeling of spaciousness where there was none before.

Doing this involved knocking down partition walls, and installing a clear glass fire screen between the kitchen and sitting room to maximise the feeling of space. There is also a fire curtain between the kitchen and the entrance area, in order to satisfy fire regulations. A sinuous corridor includes an upholstered bench for reading and a stopping point for putting on shoes. A screen to the bathroom incorporates some cast-glass Lalique figures that the client already owned – this really is a personal project.

Storage has been carefully considered, with a warm cherry veneer used in the main rooms and a sprayed white finish in the kitchen. There are coffered ceilings between downstand beams to give as much height as possible. All pipework and servicing are hidden away cleverly, and curved corners that are in keeping with the ocean-liner feel also prevent painful bumps in tight spaces. Mirrors on bulkheads increase the sense of space.

Every element has been designed for a luxurious feeling. The brass ironmongery was specially designed, using water-jet cutting and folding techniques that made it more affordable than some off-the-peg solutions. In somewhere this compact, every element and every square inch counts.

◀

1.31 LOOKING ALONG THE CURVED CORRIDOR TOWARDS THE BEDROOM. ON THE LEFT IS THE BATHROOM, WITH THE SCREEN THAT INCORPORATES LALIQUE GLASS.

◄
1.32 CHERRY JOINERY IN
THE BEDROOM.

▲
1.33 THE CORRIDOR,
INCLUDING THE
READING BENCH.

The clients said, 'We were very impressed with how the architects looked at it very imaginatively and creatively. They created the most space for storage you could ever have. Everything has been thought through – it's incredible.

Their contacts were so important. They picked a really good builder, and they knew where to go to get the wood. We were really impressed by the quality of the work.'

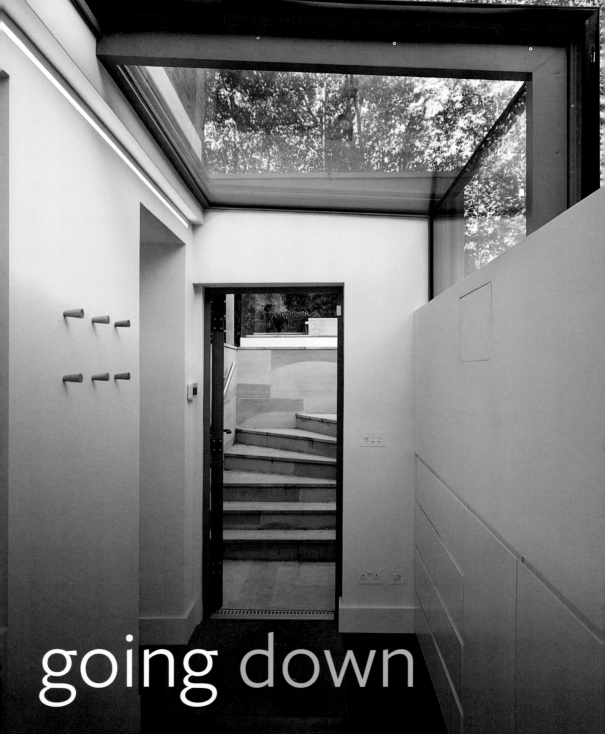

going down

2

Planning restrictions may prevent a client adding an extra floor, or they may not want to sacrifice too much of their garden space. In this case, creating or enlarging a basement may be the best solution. Basements have also become popular because people want more 'downstairs' space. They may not have large families, and may not need a lot of bedrooms, but the various functions they need their house to perform may put space on lower floors at a premium. Of course, it is usually easy to turn a spare bedroom into a home office, but many may prefer to work on the ground floor. In addition, people now want generous kitchens where older houses may have had restricted ones. And home gyms and cinemas are well suited to basement or semi-basement spaces.

At the start of the Covid-19 pandemic, when gyms closed for a considerable amount of time, sales of fitness equipment for the home rose. For some people, this may simply mean an exercise bike or a running machine, but others are more ambitious. In 2020, for example, sales of exercise bikes in the UK rose by more than 2,000% (i.e. 20-fold) and sales of weight benches and steppers went up even higher.[1] In fact, sales of all fitness equipment rocketed. Some of these people, of course, will be going back to the gym, but many will at least take a hybrid approach to fitness – they have the equipment, so why not use it at home? And all this stuff takes up space. A basement is an ideal place to put it.

But building or extending a basement is not something to be undertaken lightly. It requires excavation, which is messy, and a good understanding of structural and ground engineering. Basements need either to be tanked or to be pumped out. There are existing homes with 'flood cellars' which are expected to flood. Owners of these will, if sensible, not store anything there that could be damaged by damp, or at least keep items on high shelves. But this is not what most people are looking for if investing in new basements.

London has the largest number of basements, and particularly of 'mega-basements'. Research by Professor Roger Burrows at Newcastle University found that 7,000 basements were built or extended in London between 2008 and 2019. Of these, more than 1,500 qualify as 'mega-basements', extending under gardens or even under the street.[2] These have not been universally popular – there are potential problems with flooding, changed acoustics and, of course, the sheer disruption caused by construction. There are worries that parts of London are being 'hollowed out'.

A basement, of course, doesn't have to be this ambitious, and it may well be the best solution. Just be aware of what you are getting into. More than any other type of construction, basements can be held up by unexpected setbacks. A basement will not be cheap. And its environmental footprint is considerable. But, knowing all this, if it is the best solution for you, and your architect is confident, then go for it.

Rather than a 'mega-basement', you may just want to dig out a small enclosure, for a specific purpose. One of the projects in this chapter has a compact wine cellar beneath the kitchen. While still challenging, it is a less ambitious undertaking.

And digging down may not involve constructing a basement at all. Two of the projects shown here have floors that were lowered in order to increase headroom – both kitchens, in fact, but the same approach could be used elsewhere. Although still disruptive and demanding, this is not nearly as large a commitment as hollowing out an entire floor.

2.1 HIGHBURY HOUSE
BASEMENT BY
APPLETON WEINER,
SEE PAGE 40.

Work(out)
from Home

ARCHITECT: SCENARIO ARCHITECTURE

LOCATION: LONDON

BUDGET: £520,000

PROJECT FINISHED: 2021

◄

2.2 LOOKING FROM
THE SEATING AREA
DOWN TOWARDS THE
KITCHEN AND OUT TO
THE GARDEN.

►

2.3 THE BASEMENT
GYM HAS PLENTY OF
HEADROOM.

There are few things more irritating for somebody who likes to lift weights than restricted headroom. This became a major consideration when Scenario Architecture was asked to redesign this home for a personal trainer and a weightlifting enthusiast. The architect wanted to completely refurbish and rethink the existing spaces. The property had a typical Victorian arrangement of smaller rooms and split floors from front to back. And while the basement was the obvious place for the gym, it just wasn't deep enough. In addition, the clients wanted greater connectivity – to communicate between spaces, rather than being shut away in individual rooms.

The architect, therefore, took a fairly radical approach, taking away the whole of the original rear wall of the house and also digging down. This created space for a gym with decent head height and, behind it, a cinema that links by steps to the kitchen. These steps, in two different materials to differentiate between functions, curve round to create additional seating in the cinema area.

The architect said, 'The pandemic reinforced the client's desire to create a sanctuary at home for cooking, entertaining, daily exercise and watching films.'

A large skylight above the kitchen area, plus the fact that the new rear wall is almost entirely glazed, means that this is now a light-filled space. In addition, the wall between the raised front room and the kitchen has been replaced with a half-height glass screen, connecting the two. The result is a connected group of spaces that flow together through three levels, allowing distinct activities, but without isolation.

And the changes did not stop at this level. The architect also renovated the upper floors and created a new loft space. This was challenging because of the complexity of the original roof structure and the prominent corner position. By creating not the usual one but two dormers, and carefully positioning skylights, the architect was able to create a loft that provides a bright and luxurious guest bedroom and en suite.

2.4 THIS PHOTO SHOWS
THE THREE LEVELS: THE
CINEMA, KITCHEN AND
SITTING ROOM, ALL
CONNECTED.

**The architect wanted to completely
refurbish and rethink the existing spaces.**

2.5 THE STEPS UP FROM
THE CINEMA CAN ALSO
BE USED FOR SEATING.
THE SURFACE MATERIAL
CHANGES AS ONE MOVES
TOWARDS THE KITCHEN.

Highbury House Basement

ARCHITECT: APPLETON WEINER

LOCATION: LONDON

BUDGET: £250,000

PROJECT FINISHED: 2018

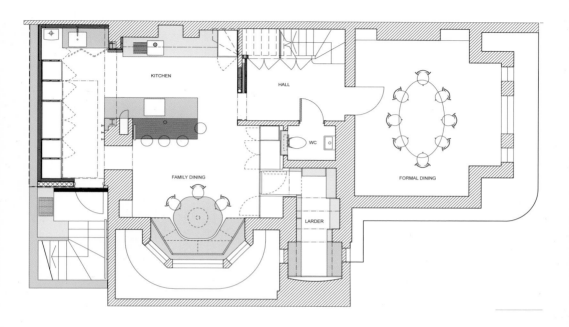

KITCHEN

HALL

WC

FORMAL DINING

FAMILY DINING

LARDER

2.6 PLAN SHOWING
THE LAYOUT OF THE
BASEMENT, WITH ITS
EXTENSION.

2.7 THE NEW
EXTENSION IS ONLY
JUST VISIBLE FROM
OUTSIDE.

Owners of family homes sometimes find they do not have enough space at lower levels. This was the case for the owners of a listed house in Highbury, in the north London borough of Islington. And, in particular, they wanted better access to outside space, both for a gardening parent and for two young boys. Appleton Weiner have provided this with an extension that is so discreet it is barely visible, almost all of it being below ground level.

In this case, the clients found the architect by personal recommendation – both families had children at the same school. The architect designed a relatively modest side extension which added only 12m² of living space, but was transformative. It sits under the driveway and only rises a little above ground level. It is intended to be reminiscent of the coal vaults that sat below the pavements of Victorian houses.

Because there is glazing to both the top of the extension and the small vertical element, it brings a lot more light into the space. The original basement had a kitchen and a dining room as well as utility room, and only a modest lightwell. The new arrangement allows for both a family eating space and a formal dining room, and has much more open access to the garden. Between the external steps and the basement enclosure is a permanent barbecue that can be used in all weathers.

Materials are deliberately neutral and subtle. The project was finished before the Covid-19 pandemic but the design seemed almost prescient. After the lockdown, the clients said it had been a 'life-saver' for home-schooling.

The architect designed a relatively modest side extension which added only 12m² of living space, but was transformative.

◄
2.10 INSIDE THE BASEMENT. IT WAS A GODSEND DURING THE PERIOD OF HOME-SCHOOLING.

▼
2.8 THE ADDITIONAL GLAZING BRINGS MORE LIGHT INTO THE BASEMENT.

Oak Brow

ARCHITECT: ANNABELLE TUGBY ARCHITECTS

LOCATION: STYAL, CHESHIRE

BUDGET: £300,000

PROJECT FINISHED: 2020

This project is a bit of a cheat because it is not a house for a client but an architect's own house. But, as Annabelle Tugby, architect and client for the project, said, 'All the elements around brief, budget and end-user requirements were, if anything, more important as we were designing for the most exacting client we've met!'

Tugby bought the rural cottage at Styal, Cheshire, from a couple who had lived there happily for 40 years. She told *The Modern House Journal*, 'I had a lovely insight into the way that they'd enjoyed the house together over the course of 40 years, but also as part of their daily routine. It felt like they'd had a very happy, romantic life here.

'I think I thought that everything that they'd set up in the house was the right answer because they'd lived here so long. It was just done in their way. When we renovated it, I was very mindful of the ways they had used the house, and their patterns and routines moving around it. So, I recreated things in specific places.'[3]

This included the booth in the kitchen, where the owners used to sit at a small round table to make the most of the sun, and also the window seat in the bathroom, where they used to chat with a G&T at the end of the day.

However, as Tugby's family grew, they needed more space, and so she came up with a plan to create this and fit the home to modern living, without destroying its character – indeed by enhancing it.

The work included a new roof and also digging out and underpinning an area of floor to create a large, modern kitchen. This may seem like a lot of work, but the low

2.11 THE HOUSE, WITH THE NEW ADDITION TO THE LEFT.

2.12 THE BOOTH IN THE KITCHEN IS IN THE PLACE WHERE THE PREVIOUS OWNERS LOVED TO SIT. NOTE THE DELIBERATELY UNFINISHED CEILING.

ceiling heights of traditional cottages don't lend themselves easily to generous modern open spaces. Digging down was the only way to achieve this additional ceiling height. This new kitchen replaced what Tugby described as 'a warren of rooms'. It has glazed doors opening to the garden.

Another change was the addition of a large, pitched-roof green oak frame to the existing 1980s flat-roof extension. Green oak, which will twist a little and crack as it seasons naturally, gives an appropriately rustic look to an area that serves both as a greenhouse and as a sheltered outdoor space.

There were also changes on the first floor. The architect removed a family bathroom, which allowed her to create a landing library instead. She then designed an en suite for each of the four bedrooms. Back on the ground floor, she created a games room for the family from an underused space beyond the utility room.

Alongside the spatial changes, the architect also greatly increased the insulation and put in a modern heating system.

Much of the success of the project relies on the thought that has gone into materials. This includes both refurbished and existing materials. Tugby refurbished all the doors and windows. In addition, in the course of restoration several elements were uncovered and reused, including all the hardware and the crook frame post in the kitchen. Much of the original ceiling in the kitchen is also exposed.

> 2.13 IN ORDER TO ACHIEVE A DECENT HEAD HEIGHT IN THE MODERN KITCHEN, TUGBY HAD TO DIG DOWN TO LOWER THE FLOOR.

2.14 THE KITCHEN
BEFORE THE BUILDING
WORKS.

Wherever possible, new materials were natural ones, such as lime plaster, seagrass flooring and reused bricks. There are a lot of cobbled paths in the area, so Tugby chose to use cobbles outside and then, in an unusual move, brought the material into the kitchen as well.

Asked if she had any guidance for clients working on similar projects, she said, 'Always check the orientation for sunlight and make early enquiries with an architect as to the feasibility of the work and the potential opportunities offered by the house. Good architects will listen to their client's needs but also to the building they are adapting. Working to retain a mood can be as important as thinking about the functionality.'

In this case, Tugby was not changing the shape, and so instead she concentrated her efforts on the surfaces, and also on the lighting scheme, where she spent a lot of time and effort. For example, she used cobbled paths around the house, inspired by local history. (There are cobbled paths throughout the village, including the path leading up to the school, which is in the area owned by the National Trust and where there is no electric lighting.)

Since Tugby was creating entirely new garden paths, instead of using concrete as there had been before, she made all her paths from pebbles. And, she said, 'It felt natural to carry that on inside.'

Tugby came up with a plan to fit the home to modern living, without destroying its character.

2.15 THE GREEN OAK
FRAME PROVIDES A
SUITABLY RUSTIC FEEL
FOR A GLASSHOUSE
AND OUTSIDE ROOM.

Caroline Place

ARCHITECT: GROUPWORK
LOCATION: LONDON
BUDGET: £500,000
PROJECT FINISHED: 2016

2.16 TRAVERTINE HAS BEEN USED WIDELY AND IN A NUMBER OF TEXTURES, AS SEEN HERE IN THE FLOORING ON THE GROUND FLOOR AND THE SPIRAL STAIRCASE TO THE RIGHT.

2.17 BUILT IN THE 1950S, THE HOUSE LOOKS LARGELY UNCHANGED FROM THE OUTSIDE.

This is not the project to emulate if you are working with a modest budget. Architect Amin Taha, founder of Groupwork which designed it, said, when asked about the cost, 'I can't quite remember, I think it was about £500,000.' But goodness, this was money well spent, transforming a property into somewhere memorable and innovative yet extremely flexible and liveable.

The degree of alteration doesn't immediately strike you when you arrive at the building, since from the outside it is almost entirely unchanged. Caroline Place is a quiet enclave of late 1950s terraces north of Hyde Park and Kensington Gardens. Internally, it harked back to an earlier period, following the Edwardian tradition of having served and servant areas,

with maids' rooms, sculleries, coal houses and a working yard. In contrast, the clients wanted an open-plan and flexible way of living.

The clients are a married couple with three children. Amin Taha knew the wife because they were at school together, and she asked Amin to carry out this radical refurbishment. Early explorations revealed the existence of travertine flooring, and of densely plastered walls behind pine boarding that had been added later.

Groupwork decided to work with these materials. Travertine is versatile, capable of being used both internally and externally and in a range of finishes, from quarry-tooled to polished. Particularly notable is the spiral staircase that runs up through the house. The stairs are smooth on the walking surface, but rough-cut underneath. There is even a travertine champagne bench in the garden, with a deliberately rough appearance and a dedicated receptacle for ice and a bottle.

The design is based on having as many clear spaces as possible. To simplify the building, the architect removed downstand beams and brick nibs. Spaces are then defined mostly by cherry-wood cabinets, rather than by walls. The most ingenious example of this is on the first floor, which can operate as a single reception area with a corner for a study. However, two full-height bookcases can swing round and unfold to enclose the study entirely. And, if an extra bed is needed, there is one that can fold down from one of these cabinets. Other cabinets in the house define bathrooms, wardrobes and laundry rooms.

The other two materials that are used widely are concrete and brass. For example, the soffit of the basement, which was cast

in concrete, has been exposed and bush-hammered to give it a deliberately rough finish. This basement provides not only a music room and family room, but also a utility room below the garage/study in a separate building, linked at basement level. Brass, in a variety of finishes, has been used for lighting, on doors, on taps and handrails and on basins and WCs. There is even a brass chain-mail shower curtain.

As part of the project, windows were all replaced, and walls and the roof were insulated, greatly improving the thermal performance.

Amin Taha described a working relationship that was deliberately based on trust, rather than detailed involvement. He said, 'A lot of trust was put into our hands, also meaning the client was less emotionally involved with every detail, which is often the failure of so many private house projects. The result being on time, budget and if sold on completion a 40% profit on costs.'

His advice for clients is to avoid emotional involvement on every detail. He said, 'Do not insist on attending every meeting with every consultant and contractor and supplier. No consultant or contractor attempts that level of control and involvement; you will have a nervous breakdown thinking you need to decide it all and in doing so only drive up consultant fees in them repeatedly redrawing every option, resulting in a building that is over time, budget and now a miserable physical reminder of your folly. Set out your brief, hand over some material ideas if you really insist on them, then leave it to the professionals to handle day to day. It'll be a wonderful delight of spaces and details.'

There are many clients who would be nervous about this approach, but it certainly worked here. The husband, who is a hedge-fund manager, has given the practice a number of other, larger projects to look at.

2.18 CHERRY WOOD HAS BEEN USED WIDELY FOR FURNITURE THAT ACTS AS ROOM DIVIDERS. ON THE FIRST FLOOR, THESE UNITS CAN SWING ROUND TO PROVIDE DIFFERENT ARRANGEMENTS.

2.19 THERE IS A FOLD-OUT BED IN ONE OF THE UNITS.

2.20 HAMMERED CONCRETE PROVIDES A DELIBERATELY ROUGH FINISH TO THE BASEMENT SOFFIT.

The clients wanted an open-plan and flexible way of living.

Old Redford Cottage

ARCHITECT: RX ARCHITECTS

LOCATION: PEASMARSH, RYE, EAST SUSSEX

BUDGET: £190,000 PLUS FEES & VAT

PROJECT FINISHED: 2019

How do you turn a 16th-century thatched farm cottage into a modern home? RX Architects managed this feat in Peasmarsh, East Sussex, by adding a new extension to the side, joined with a glazed link. While the two parts match well externally, they have a very different feel internally – the traditional cottage, with its low ceilings, beams and leaded windows, is relatively dark and has restricted views of the garden.

In contrast, the new extension is light and open. It has been dug down into the ground so that it sits more comfortably in the garden. The roof level is the same as on the original cottage, disguising the additional height that makes it more airy.

The clients, who found their architect via a recommendation from a satisfied customer, wanted additional living and sleeping accommodation. The extension includes a new guest suite with bedroom, bathroom and dressing area within the roof pitch, with large dormers looking out across the gardens. The stairs that lead up there are set behind a wall at the rear of the kitchen.

Beautifully crafted in wood, they feel like another piece of kitchen furniture.

Externally, the two buildings sit comfortably together thanks to the detailing on the new addition, which both complements and contrasts with the existing building. Cladding is with bleached white larch on the extension, matching the cladding on the original cottage. But whereas on the original, the cladding runs horizontally, on the extension it is vertical on the lower floor. It changes to horizontal on the upper floor, in line with the place where the thatch on the cottage dips down.

This is an unusual approach to creating additional space, and one that works well. A thatched cottage is a simple and complete object that rarely takes well to extension. By creating, effectively, a separate building, albeit one that is linked by an 'invisible' corridor, the architect has worked in the tradition of farm buildings that are often grouped together, while creating something that is unmistakably of today.

This is an unusual approach to creating
additional space, and one that works well.

2.23 A RADICAL
SOLUTION BUT
ONE THAT WORKS
IN CONTEXT:
THE EXTENSION
SITS ALONGSIDE
THE ORIGINAL
COTTAGE.

2.24 THE STAIRS TO
THE UPPER FLOOR
ARE ELEGANTLY
CONCEALED BEHIND
THE NEW KITCHEN.

2.25 DEFINITELY NOT
'COTTAGECORE' – THE
NEW KITCHEN IS
SIMPLE, MODERN AND
ELEGANT.

The Nook

ARCHITECT: STUDIO 163
LOCATION: LONDON
BUDGET: UNDER £100,000
PROJECT FINISHED: 2020

2.26 THE WINDOW NOOK IS A GREAT PLACE FOR LOOKING OUT – OR READING, WHEN FAMILY LIFE ALLOWS.

2.27 THE WINE CELLAR IS HIDDEN BENEATH THE KITCHEN FLOOR.

They needed a more open space where the family could be together.

The kitchen of this house in Lambeth, south London, holds a surprise. The floor opens up, and there are stairs that lead down to a wine cellar. This is the most unusual aspect of a project that otherwise aimed to provide the clients with a modest extension that would better reflect the way we live today.

What they had was a narrow galley kitchen with an extension beyond it that acted as a dining room. They needed a more open space where the family could be together, and that had a better connection to the garden. And they wanted a wine cellar.

They found the architect, Studio 163, through a recommendation from a friend. The solution was to extend the extension, widening the kitchen space and allowing the kitchen and dining area to function as a single room. A 'window nook' at the end

serves a number of purposes and is key to the transformation of the space. It acts as a secluded place to read and overlook the garden; it forms an end seat to the breakfast table; and it has storage underneath for the children's toys.

There was not enough money in the budget for a fully bespoke kitchen. Instead, the architect suggested using inexpensive units and putting on bespoke doors, which give the desired effect at lesser cost. The continuous splashback in the kitchen is a subtle terrazzo finish.

The architect said, 'The wine cellar was probably the most challenging part of the build as the space was relatively small and everything had to be really precise to position the cellar and its underpinning. This introduced significant excavation works.'

2.28 BUILDING THE
WINE CELLAR WAS
CHALLENGING, BUT
WAS AN ESSENTIAL
PART OF THE CLIENTS'
BRIEF.

And they had this advice for future clients, 'On this sort of project, it is always better if the design process is hand in hand with the client as it needs to serve their daily life purpose and their aesthetic, but as architects our purpose is to challenge them and bring some ideas to the table that they might not have thought of in the first place. This also means that the relationship between client and architect is key.

'Do not be worried as well about smaller budgets; it can open up some creative ideas or use of materials.'

The relationship certainly worked in this case. Studio 163 is now embarking on a loft extension and reconfiguring the upper levels of the house.

2.29 LOOKING IN FROM
OUTSIDE – THE HOUSE IS
MUCH BETTER CONNECTED
TO THE GARDEN NOW.

2.30 THE SLEEK KITCHEN
HAS STANDARD UNITS
WITH BESPOKE FRONTS.

special places

3

Some buildings lend themselves to relatively standard solutions. For instance, a lot of semidetached and terraced Victorian houses in cities and suburbs have rear extensions with a narrow strip of land to one side. Filling in this side return is a relatively easy way to get more space and the broader space which allows for flexible living, with rooms flowing into each other.

The solution is not off the shelf, since every house and every family have their own quirks. Design skill is needed to deal with these. But the answers, although sometimes elegant or even beautiful, are rarely surprising.

And then there are the other buildings. For one reason or another, they don't fit the mould. The clients may want to create something different. Or they may be starting from an unusual position, with an eccentric building.

All the projects in this chapter fit those categories. Three of them are entirely within an existing building envelope, showing that, with the right expertise, you can truly make something from nothing – or at least have the impression of more space even if the absolute figures for square footage show that is not the case. You may not want to install a library in a two-bedroom house, or turn a high-rise flat into a Japanese sanctuary, but these projects should show you at least that dreams can come true. And though no project is cheap in absolute terms, remodelling rather than extending will certainly save you money.

Other projects shown here are odd or difficult buildings, which have had troubled histories and need a rethink. Again, the solution is the opposite of an off-the-shelf answer. Here, more than anywhere else, it is essential to find the right architect. By definition they are unlikely to have done anything exactly like this. What you are looking for is an architect whose approach you like, who you feel is in sympathy with your aspirations and who has done other work that appeals to you. These should, of course, always be the criteria when choosing an architect, but with this type of project it is more important than ever.

These are projects for which there is no predefined roadmap. That might make them scary, even daunting, but oh so exciting. If you and your architect can carry off one of these (and there is no reason why you shouldn't), then you will be a very fortunate client indeed.

◄
3.1 AMHURST ROAD
BY POULSOM
MIDDLEHURST, SEE
PAGE 62.

Amhurst
Road

ARCHITECT: POULSOM MIDDLEHURST

LOCATION: LONDON

BUDGET: £107,300 (CONSTRUCTION COST ONLY)

PROJECT FINISHED: 2017

◄
3.2 THE NEW STEEL
STRUCTURE IS A
STRONG GREEN
COLOUR, BECOMING A
FEATURE RATHER THAN
DISGUISED.

Sometimes an extension is the answer to a problem, but in other cases there is neither the need nor the money to build one. The latter was the case with a two-storey maisonette on the basement and ground floor of a four-storey Victorian terrace in Hackney, east London.

The rooms, which were large with high ceilings, were suited to the original single Victorian house but felt underutilised in the current maisonette. The owners wanted to add a bedroom and to combine their living areas into one larger single space, rather than the original sprawl over separate floors. They asked for an open and playful heart in the centre of the house for friends and family to enjoy.

As part of the works, a central load-bearing wall was removed to allow an open-plan living and kitchen area overlooking the garden. The beam that replaces the wall is a strong green colour, forming a feature rather than being disguised.

Originally, there was a large but dark hall-way. The architects reduced this in width to allow for the creation of a new en-suite shower room to the downstairs bedroom. A bespoke staircase now sits centrally in the space, improving the circulation. It has open timber treads and a balustrade of slats in a simple geometric pattern, allowing light to come down through it and providing an additional sense of space.

▶
3.3 LOOKING IN FROM
THE GARDEN.

'The main challenge,' said the architects, 'was to meet our client's budget whilst creating the look and feel they wanted for their space. In order to manage costs, we agreed mini budgets for each aspect of the project so that they could select suitable fittings and finishes to meet their targets. They rose to the challenge and put a lot of research into getting the look they wanted for the budget they had. They accepted compromises they had to make to achieve this, one of which was to phase the bespoke joinery they had planned for their living space.

'Our advice is to spend some time getting clear on your priorities at the outset of your project. This will give you a structure by which to make those difficult decisions through the design and build stages. It's good to remember that compromise is a result of managing a project successfully!'

The owners wanted an open and playful heart in the centre of the house for friends and family to enjoy.

3.4 THE SPACE CAN LEND ITSELF TO A VARIETY OF USES.

3.5 THE PROJECT
INCLUDES A NEW
BATHROOM.

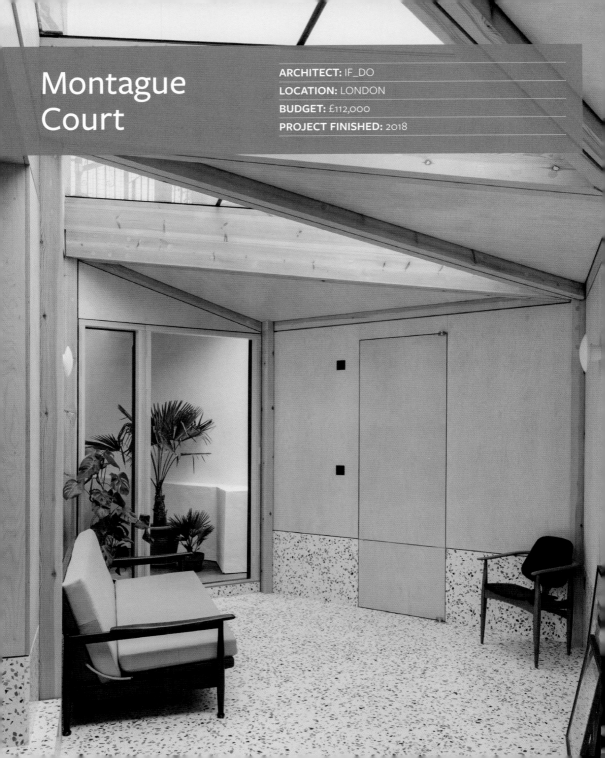

Montague Court

ARCHITECT: IF_DO

LOCATION: LONDON

BUDGET: £112,000

PROJECT FINISHED: 2018

◄

3.6 THE FLITCHED
BEAMS (TIMBER WITH
STEEL INSERTIONS)
FORM AN INTERESTING
PATTERN.

Forget everything you know about extensions when looking at this project. It could not be further from a typical rear extension, but then it was not a typical flat to begin with. This apartment, in Hackney, east London, is on the ground floor of a converted former synagogue, a building that was octagonal in plan. The living room was, in part, a double-height space, but the owners wanted more room. They had an awkward-shaped external space, sandwiched between the building and an enclosing wall and roughly following the angles of the building. It was pretty scruffy and not used for much more than bicycle storage and some ad hoc seating.

The clients found the architect, IF_DO, through a mutual friend and gave the practice a brief to create a flexible new space they could use for working from home and that could, occasionally, serve as an extra bedroom.

The architect came up with a solution that retained only the southern, sunnier part of the garden. The rest is occupied by an extension with a triangulated plan that responds to the unusual geometry and sits between the existing walls of the building and the site boundary. Seven exposed timber posts support the bespoke metal flitch plates and deep softwood joists that make up the triangular panels of the roof. Large

With a relatively small flat like this, every additional usable space is valuable.

►

3.7 THE SPACE INTO
WHICH THE EXTENSION
WAS BUILT WAS NOT
VALUED.

rooflights bring north light into the space. In addition to the new workroom, there is also a small utility room, tucked into a corner and accessed from the bedroom. With a relatively small flat like this, every additional usable space is valuable.

Constructing the extension was not easy as there was no external access. Everything had to be carried by hand through a narrow, shared corridor, and no element could be more than 2.4m long or it would not have got in. This meant that there had to be additional connections to achieve the longer spans needed.

The architect has lined the extension with timber and given it a terrazzo floor. Both finishes extend through the entire flat, transforming somewhere that felt rather like a student flat into a bright, contemporary, light-filled space with that all-important extra accommodation.

◄ 3.8 LOOKING THROUGH FROM THE KITCHEN TO THE EXTENSION. ALL THE CONSTRUCTION ELEMENTS HAD TO COME THROUGH THE BUILDING.

◄ 3.9 FINISHES OF TIMBER AND TERRAZZO PROVIDE A SIMPLE, CONTEMPORARY FEEL. LIGHT REACHES THE EXTENSION THROUGH THE TRIANGULAR GLAZED PANELS.

► 3.10 THE NEW EXIT TO THE GARDEN.

The Old School

ARCHITECT: ARKLEBOYCE

LOCATION: HOWSHAM, NORTH YORKSHIRE

BUDGET: £250,000

PROJECT FINISHED: 2018

ArkleBoyce have photos of the students and teachers at the old schoolhouse in Howsham which forms the basis of this project. The building is surprisingly small (village schools were) but attractive, with its symmetrical frontage and two Gothic-arched windows. It was rebuilt in 1852 and is, not surprisingly, Grade II listed. The hamlet in which it sits is a conservation area and is part of an Area of Outstanding Natural Beauty.

However, everything behind the original building had been neglected. ArkleBoyce therefore came up with a proposal to reorder and extend the living space to create a contemporary extension, providing a series of interconnecting spaces, with panoramic views of the garden and the landscape beyond. As well as the drama of the view, this allowed the parents to keep an eye on their children when they were playing outside.

A glazed link joins the unchanged existing building to a new and contrasting extension. It is mostly single storey, and the glazing opens dramatically on one corner, which is only supported on a single column. This long room acts as a kitchen-diner, with a playroom behind it. A corridor doubles as a storage space. This ground-floor extension is clad in stone, referencing dry-stone walls and echoing the rock-faced limestone façade of the schoolhouse.

◀

3.11 THE LARGE
GROUND-FLOOR
EXTENSION, WITH THE
SMALL TIMBER-CLAD
EXTENSION ABOVE.

3.12 SEEN FROM THE FRONT, THE OLD
SCHOOL BUILDING IS CHARMING, BUT IT
WAS NEGLECTED BEHIND.
▼

There is also a smaller extension on the first floor, containing an additional bedroom and an en-suite bathroom. Clad in timber, this references Yorkshire boarded agricultural barns.

Changes to the original building had to be minimal, but remodelled areas and the new extension provide high levels of thermal mass and airtightness. The house now has a biomass boiler and a green roof on the single-floor extension, both giving improved environmental credentials.

The architect said, 'It is important not to rush to a solution; live in a property and understand the challenges and constraints fully to ensure the end result satisfies your needs. Employ a full design team and engage with them in order to have a robust set of information prior to starting on site, helping to minimise challenges wherever possible.'

▲
3.13 CHANGES TO THE ORIGINAL
BUILDING HAD TO BE MINIMAL,
BUT THE STANDARDS OF
INSULATION HAVE IMPROVED.

▲
3.14 ARCHED DOORWAYS
ARE ONE OF THE CHARMING
FEATURES OF THE ORIGINAL
BUILDING.

3.15 INSIDE THE FIRST-FLOOR EXTENSION.

'It is important not to rush to a solution; live in a property and understand the challenges and constraints fully.'

Samarkand

ARCHITECT: NAPIER CLARKE ARCHITECTS
LOCATION: GREAT MISSENDEN, BUCKINGHAMSHIRE
BUDGET: CONFIDENTIAL
PROJECT FINISHED: 2019

3.16 THE EXTENSION
IS NOW CLAD IN
CHARRED WOOD,
SEPARATED FROM
THE REST OF THE
HOUSE BY A GLAZED
ENTRANCE.

Look at this house in Little Kingshill, on the outskirts of Great Missenden, Buckinghamshire, and your first impression will be of a 1970s house joined to a more modern extension by a glazed entrance. You won't be far wrong. There is an extension, but it has not been added in a recent refurbishment. The charred-wood cladding may be utterly contemporary, but the extension itself long predates it. And the glazed entrance *is* new, but it was carved out from the existing building, not added on.

This means that the amount of new building is far less than one may assume at first glance. Napier Clarke Architects consciously looked at the existing building and at the client's needs, and questioned whether the house could be refurbished rather than replaced. One of the architects said, 'For this project we really believed that we could work with the original house, creating a highly sustainable project through the virtue of retaining the existing. The client was keen to retain the existing if it was more cost-effective than rebuilding.

3.17 WHEN THE
CURRENT OWNERS
BOUGHT THE HOUSE, IT
ALREADY HAD A RATHER
UNSYMPATHETIC
EXTENSION.

The client also has an environmental conscience and was keen to explore this route, recognising the sustainable benefits of doing so.'

The brief therefore was to create a contemporary family home that would help to prolong the life of the original house. While the footprint stayed the same, space was won by using the former garage, which was in the extension, as living space and by arranging the interior more effectively. The entrance moved to a position between the extension and the original building, previously used as a utility room.

Most of the extension is now a kitchen and dining area, with the rest occupied by a utility room. The living areas in the original house, which previously included the kitchen, have also been rearranged, and there is a new staircase that better suits the new circulation arrangements. With open treads and bannisters, this cuts out as little light as possible, and looks dramatic when seen through the windows.

On the upper floor, the number of bedrooms has been reduced from six to four. The extension now houses the master bedroom, with an en-suite bathroom and a dressing room, and there is a new family bathroom in the main part of the building that is larger than any of the previous bathrooms.

The house is in the greenbelt, but there was no issue in relation to this because the house was not enlarged. However, it is also in the Chiltern Area of Outstanding Natural Beauty, which states that any 'proposal should conserve, where practicable and appropriate, and enhance'. So the architect needed to demonstrate to the local planning authority that the new materials and design would do this. The planners were, said the architect, supportive throughout the pre-application and planning application process.

As well as the rearrangement and new appearance of rooms, the architect insulated the ground floor, first floor and roof to reduce thermal loss. They changed all the windows and doors from single-glazed to double-glazed and replaced the heating system with underfloor heating on the ground floor and radiators on the first floor. This means that the house not only looks different and is different to live in, it also behaves differently, in tune with the energy concerns of today.

▶ 3.18 THE KITCHEN AND DINING AREA IN THE EXTENSION.

The brief was to create a contemporary family home that would help to prolong the life of the original house.

▲
3.19 THE NEW
STAIRCASE ALLOWS
LIGHT TO PENETRATE
THE GROUND FLOOR.

▶
3.20 THE UPPER
FLOOR HAS ALSO
BEEN ENTIRELY
REARRANGED.

Shakespeare Tower

ARCHITECT: TAKERO SHIMAZAKI ARCHITECTS

LOCATION: LONDON

BUDGET: CONFIDENTIAL

PROJECT FINISHED: 2019

◄ 3.21 OVERVIEW OF THE INTERIOR. NOTE THE NON-STRUCTURAL TERRAZZO COLUMN IN THE REAR, WITH THE TATAMI ROOM TO THE LEFT OF IT.

➤ 3.22 SHAKESPEARE TOWER AT THE BARBICAN IS NOT WHERE ONE WOULD EXPECT TO FIND A JAPANESE APARTMENT.

The client said, 'We did not care much for what has become the standard "modernist" open-plan look of recent Barbican flat renovations, in which everything is revealed the moment one steps in, like a New York loft or a WeWork office. We were more interested in things which are occluded, blocked, hidden, only to be discovered gradually. A completely stripped-out and empty flat looks strangely small. Screens, panels, columns, sliding doors, blinds: all these paradoxically add space by imposing structure.'

The architect followed these wishes, taking what had been a two-bedroom apartment and opening it up, using screens instead of walls. The client had deliberately bought a flat in which the end balcony had already been enclosed (this was not possible after the building was listed in 2001) and so had a little more space to play with.

The architect stripped out the flat entirely, in most cases replacing internal walls and doors with screens and columns, using floor texture to delineate different areas. Strips of terrazzo outline the main areas, with grey carpet within them. There is an almost cobbled floor of inset stones in the entrance area, tiling in the kitchen space and bathroom, and tatami mats (the only touch of warm colour on the floors) in the 'Japanese room'.

There is also a terrazzo-clad column used at a key transition point in the space. This looks at first sight like a piece of the building structure, but in fact the architect inserted this for visual effect and it serves no structural purpose. The ceilings in all the main living rooms are lined in strips of solid cherry. Walls have been finished in a

Look at the Shakespeare Tower, one of the markers of the Barbican Centre, designed by Chamberlin, Powell and Bon, and try to imagine what the flats are like inside. It is unlikely that your imagination will stretch to a Japanese-style interior, but that is exactly what Takero Shimazaki Architects have created for a client that had lived first in Japan and later in Scandinavia, and had very strong ideas about what they wanted. This project is a great indication of how a client with definite ideas about the feeling and mood they are seeking can work closely with an architect who is in sympathy with that approach and provides the specialist design skills to realise it.

◄

3.23 THE GALLEY
KITCHEN IS SEPARATED
FROM THE REST OF
THE APARTMENT BY A
SCREEN.

This project is a great indication of how a client
with definite ideas about the feeling and mood they
are seeking can work closely with an architect who
is in sympathy with that approach

3.24 A COBBLED FLOOR DELINEATES THE ENTRANCE. NOTE THAT THE CEILING SLATS ALSO RUN IN AN OPPOSING DIRECTION TO THE MAIN SPACE.

3.25 THE NEUTRAL PALETTE CONTINUES IN THE BATHROOM, BUT IN A DARKER TONE.

clay plaster with straw binder for added highlights and texture.

The client said about this choice of materials, 'It is an accepted truism that a plain white ceiling is best for creating a feeling of space and light, mimetically alluding to the sky above us, just as wood or concrete flooring alludes to the earth below. In fact, the opposite can be true, as [Alvar] Aalto showed us in his Villa Mairea, and as t-sa [Takero Shimazaki Architects] has realised here. Dense, dark, slatted, low: precisely aligned unidirectional ceiling timber leads the eye away along the axis of the living space, creating an unexpected feeling of height and breadth. Continuing this radical inversion of the usual narrative, woven wool, the colour of pale clouds, covers the floor.'

Takero Shimazaki was born in Japan but came to the UK as a child and was educated as an architect here. He said, 'We had never designed with the language or details of traditional Japanese architecture prior to this and we enjoyed the challenge very much. Yet, against this background, we hope that our own personal and atmospheric gestures are present in the spaces.'

They certainly are. This is a London flat with Japanese influences, not a pure piece of Japanese architecture. There are two strong identities – that of the brutalist Barbican and the contemplative, Japanese-influenced interior. They work together beautifully. This is a clear example of a client with a strong feeling for the atmosphere they wanted to create, putting themselves in the hands of a talented architect.

Loft Library

ARCHITECT: ARBOREAL ARCHITECTURE
LOCATION: LONDON
BUDGET: CONFIDENTIAL
PROJECT FINISHED: 2018

◄
3.26 THE LIBRARY EVEN
INCLUDES A DESK FOR
WORKING AT.

The phrase 'books do furnish a room',
originally the title of a novel by Anthony
Powell, is bandied about. And it is true that
many rooms look better with books on the
walls. But what if you have the books, but
no, or no more, wall space for them? Then
the answer is a library. And if you don't have
a room available, perhaps you can make
one. At least this was the solution sought
by the client for this project by Arboreal
Architecture.

The client lives in a two-storey end-of-terrace house in Walthamstow, east London.
Built in the 1980s, it had brick cavity walls
and a trussed rafter roof. The single pitch
of the roof formed a space at one end
of the loft which was not easy to access
because of the diagonal members in the
timber trusses.

▲
3.27 SPRUCE PLYWOOD
HAS MORE CHARACTER
THAN BIRCH, AS WELL
AS BEING CHEAPER.

➤
3.28 COMPARE THE
HOUSE (ON THE RIGHT)
TO ITS NEIGHBOUR
(ON THE LEFT) AND
YOU CAN SEE WHERE
WINDOWS HAVE BEEN
INSERTED ON THE TOP
FLOOR.

The answer the architect came up with,
working with structural engineer Corbett
& Tasker, was to replace the diagonal truss
members with plywood arches, opening up
the space. This made it possible to incorpo-
rate 40 linear metres of book shelves, plus
a new staircase, a small bench and a study
space at the end. In total, there are 10m² of
additional floor space.

Since there was no external building work,
this fell within the client's restricted budget.
The architect chose spruce plywood rather
than birch, both because it cost less and because it has a more defined and decorative
grain. The ply is 18mm thick throughout.

In order to create the curved arches, the
architect took detailed measurements of
the existing loft space and drew templates
in CAD (computer-aided design). The CNC
(computer numerical control) service, Cut

& Construct, then cut the elements precisely to shape. It supplied these elements to the contractor with screw holes and item numbers cut into the material to ensure quick and easy assembly.

In order to bring in light, three vertical triple-glazed windows were installed on the north side, between the trussed rafters, and another window on the west elevation that catches the warm evening sun.

There were further measures to keep the cost down. The roof structure was left in place throughout the works, saving on the additional expense of rain-proofing the construction site. The architect sought quotations for the supply, cutting and delivery of the plywood arches, staircase, shelves, bench and desk before going out to tender to the main contractor, to avoid the risk that an apparently complex project would be overpriced by tendering contractors.

This project would not be the solution for everybody, but that is the point. In this particular house, for this particular client, it was exactly what was needed. The architect managed to find a solution that is exciting as well as practical and, by close control of every element, ensured it was successful and affordable.

The architect managed to find a solution that is exciting as well as practical.

Georgian House

ARCHITECT: LYNCH ARCHITECTS

LOCATION: LONDON

BUDGET: £80,000 (CONSTRUCTION COST ONLY)

PROJECT FINISHED: 2016

◄

3.31 THE BEDROOM IS
NOW AT THE REAR OF
THE BASEMENT FLOOR.
THE EXPOSED BEAMS
GIVE A FEELING OF
ADDITIONAL HEIGHT.

►

3.32 FROM THE OUTSIDE,
THE APPEARANCE OF
THE GEORGIAN HOUSE
IS UNALTERED.

Patrick and Claudia Lynch, of Lynch
Architects, restored this Georgian house
in east London for their own family. The
house is Grade II listed, and so there were
few alterations they could make to the
original fabric. But they worked with it,
largely stripping back and repairing to
celebrate the original. Most of this work
was on the fireplaces and windows.

The main change to the arrangement of the
building was that the architects moved the
kitchen from the basement to the ground
floor, where it is combined with the dining
room. Both spaces enjoy the generous
room height, good light and views over the
garden. Because the space is now open,
both morning and evening light come in.

With the basement now empty, the architects decided to use it for the master bedroom plus an en suite at the rear, and a bathroom and dressing room at the front. They increased insulation and privacy by installing an internal layer of tongue-and-groove timber lining, plus a double-glazed translucent window inside the original sash window. In order to make the space feel taller, they removed the ceiling, exposing the floor joists above.

The house had original timber and stone floors, and a stone staircase built by the original owner. All were worn but intact, and the architects kept them, celebrating the patina. They painted all the walls and built-in joinery, such as doors, shutters and skirting boards, in a single colour, as would have been done when the house was built in 1810. In most of the house, the colour is a light grey, selected to reflect the light in a gentle manner. The exceptions are the family bathroom, which is a soft greyish-green, and the children's bedrooms, which are a subtle pink.

One new element is a timber bike shelter at the bottom of the garden. Landscape designer Richard Nye redesigned the garden, which is a mix of paving and grass.

The architects said, 'Our advice to clients would be to respect the fabric and atmosphere of a house and work with what is there, to make it both simpler and richer.'

◄

3.33 THE NEW BATHROOM AT THE FRONT OF THE BASEMENT, WITH THE OBSCURED WINDOW. THE ORIGINAL STONE FLOOR HAS BEEN KEPT.

Respect the fabric and atmosphere of a house and work with what is there.

◄
3.34 THE ARCHITECTS
EXPOSED THE ORIGINAL
STONE STAIRCASE,
WITH ALL ITS WEAR
AND TEAR.

▲
3.35 THE DINING AREA
ON THE GROUND
FLOOR. ORIGINAL
ELEMENTS SUCH AS
FIREPLACES HAVE BEEN
RESTORED.

89

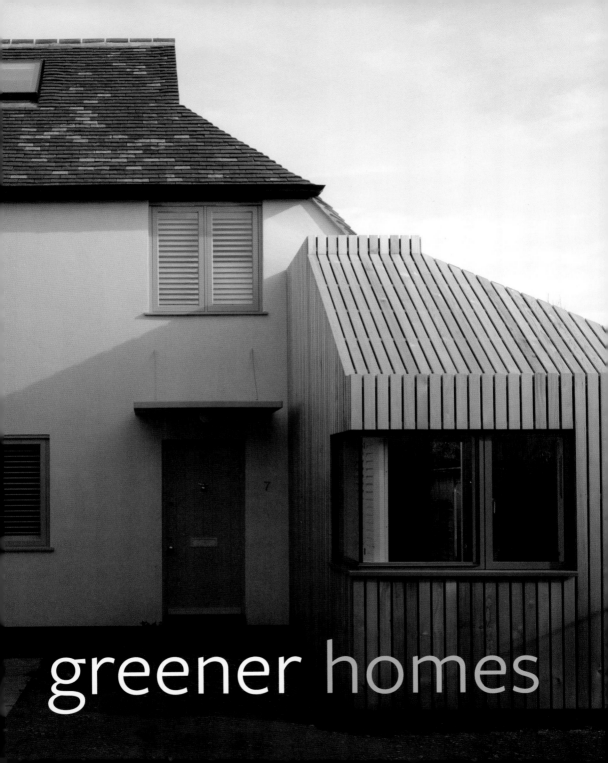

greener homes

4

If you build an extension to your house, it will almost definitely be better insulated than the original building, because building regulations will require it. And while having a well-insulated extension and a less well-insulated house is far from ideal, this should give some improvements in energy consumption.

But that is the minimum. Upgrading the rest of the house at the same time is sensible if affordable and/or practical. And it is also worth remembering that regulations only stipulate the minimum that is acceptable. You may want to do better than the minimum, either because you are worried about future energy bills, or because you care about the planet – or both. Increasing insulation levels and, crucially, looking at airtightness are two things you can do. Using renewables, such as solar panels, is another, as is the switch to electricity (which is increasingly renewable) from gas, and the installation of a heat pump.

But there is more to sustainability than that. As our homes become increasingly energy-efficient and so consume less energy, then the embodied energy becomes more significant. This is the energy that goes into making our homes – the energy in extraction of materials, in processing them, transporting them and putting them together on site. One way to minimise this is to do as little as possible – to adapt what you have and do as little new building as possible. At least one project here takes this, not to extremes, but further than most would do, repurposing materials to fulfil another function.

If this is what you care about, and you should, then you should think as well about the durability of what you are building. The energy that goes into making a building seems less worrying if you can be sure that the building will last for a very long time. You can do this both by choosing something that is inherently durable, and by avoiding the cutting edge of fashion, which may seem dated in just a few years.

And, of course, you could think about the environmental impact of your materials. Minimising the generation of carbon dioxide is vitally important, but it is not the only element of sustainability. You may want to think of the polluting potential of materials, of their scarcity, even of the conditions of those working to extract or make them. It is up to you to decide, and to find an architect who can help you, who shares your aspirations and your interests.

◄
4.1 CAMBRIDGE HOUSE
BY SAM TISDALL
ARCHITECTS, SEE
PAGE 92.

Cambridge House

ARCHITECT: SAM TISDALL ARCHITECTS

LOCATION: CAMBRIDGE

COST: CONFIDENTIAL

PROJECT FINISHED: 2020

Back extensions are common, but this house in Cambridge has a far more unusual front extension as well. This was made possible because the house had a long front garden and was set back from its neighbours. Sam Tisdall, of Sam Tisdall Architects, said, 'Because the house was arranged to the back of its site, this front extension made total sense. It was key because it allowed a really generous entrance space. This allowed a new and more generous staircase but also formed an unusual sculptural element at the front of the building. What was originally a tiny hall alongside a squeezed-in winding staircase became a room in its own right – something you would normally get only in a larger house. Although a hall seems like an insignificant room, it basically transformed the feeling of the house.'

In addition, the architect reclad a poorly built extension at the back and reconfigured it to provide a kitchen and dining space. Extending the extension upwards allowed the addition of another family bathroom and an en suite. Both the front and rear extensions are clad in cedar boarding.

As well as making the house more spacious and contemporary, the transformation made it more sustainable. In addition to new windows and a new insulated roof, the architect insulated it with a modern render system.

'This is a great way to get an insulated envelope which is equivalent to new-build standards but also means that the brick walls are thermally exposed inside,' Tisdall said. 'This thermal mass means that the internal environment is stable and comfortable.'

The client came to the architect with a brief to extend and refurbish the building. She had seen a previous project, a new house at Dorset Road in London, which had been published quite widely and wanted the same overall feel of calm and tranquillity.

There were a number of challenges. Tisdall admitted that the budget was too low at the start and 'this was compounded by us not grasping that this had not increased

◄

4.4 THE ENLARGED HALL
HAS TRANSFORMED THE
FEEL OF THE HOUSE.

4.5 THE CLIENT HAS
ACHIEVED THE SENSE
OF TRANQUILLITY SHE
WAS SEEKING.

**As well as making the house
more spacious and contemporary,
the transformation made it
more sustainable.**

sufficiently in line with the increased scope of work. This was stressful for everyone to negotiate. How to balance ambition with budget is generally the no. 1 issue that I find difficult to deal with, particularly when working with old buildings that are close to the end of their serviceable life and often need to be completely stripped back to brick.'

There are few projects that do not go at least a little way over the initial budget. As a client, it is worth asking for clarity about what things will cost. As Tisdall said, 'Expect some tricky moments and remember what you are working towards. Keep on talking.'

It is also vital to decide what really matters to you. On this project the client was adamant that, despite the need to scale back costs, she wanted to keep the Douglas fir floor that was installed in the main living areas and also on the stairs and landings. She therefore made compromises elsewhere.

If Tisdall was designing the house now, he would, he said, install an air-source heat pump instead of a gas boiler. 'It has a higher upfront cost but zero emissions on site and the renewable heat incentive (RHI) typically pays back £1–2.5k per year and, depending on particular circumstances, a payback period of perhaps 10 years or less is possible. That is, however, still a long time.'

Croft Lodge Studio

ARCHITECT: KATE DARBY ARCHITECTS AND DAVID CONNOR DESIGN

LOCATION: LEOMINSTER, HEREFORDSHIRE

BUDGET: £160,000

PROJECT FINISHED: 2018

◄

4.6 IT MAY LOOK LIKE
A WRECK BUT THAT IS
DELIBERATE – THIS IS
THE BUILDING AFTER
REFURBISHMENT.

▶

4.7 THE BUILDING HAS A
SLEEK NEW SKIN THAT
PROTECTS IT FROM THE
WEATHER.

A lot of old buildings are described as 'wrecks' but this one really was – a ruin of a 300-year-old cottage, mostly held together by ivy. Despite its appalling condition, it was within listed curtilage – this is the law that says that any structures that were built before July 1948 and are within the curtilage of a listed building have themselves to be treated as listed buildings.

In fact, Kate Darby Architects and David Connor Design, whose principals collaborated on the design, preserved this building in a literal way that few would have envisaged. This is certainly not the solution for everybody, but it is visually stunning and original.

Faced with the questions of how they could afford to restore it, and which parts were worth preserving, the pair decided to keep everything. Not just the timber frame with its carpenters' marks, but also the peeling lime plaster, the rotten timbers and even the dead ivy, the birds' nests and the dead bats.

This is not, however, what you see when you arrive at the building. Instead, you see a sleek black structure, an outer shell that is effectively a highly insulated new carapace that provides all the performance the old building could not. It consists of a steel portal frame, infilled with timber, sheeted with OSB (oriented strand board), insulated, wrapped in a waterproof membrane and clad with black corrugated iron.

Inside, however, is an enormous contrast. Set against the preserved dereliction are simple modern elements, including a stainless-steel kitchen. Two modern wood-burning stoves use timber from the surrounding forest.

There are photovoltaic panels on the roof and 100m of glycol-filled piping runs beneath the black roof surface, providing solar heating for water in the summer.

For the designers, this was, with a construction cost of £160,000, an affordable way to create a working studio with living accommodation above. They also had an eye to future uses – it has been designed so it could easily be converted into a three-bedroom house with two bathrooms. And, it is safe to say, this would be a house like no other.

◄ 4.8 'ROOM FOR IMPROVEMENT' – THE WRECK AS FOUND.

◄ 4.9 AT PRESENT, THIS IS A WORKING STUDIO, WITH LIVING SPACE ABOVE, BUT IT HAS BEEN DESIGNED SO THE WHOLE BUILDING COULD BE CONVERTED INTO A HOUSE.

► 4.10 REVELLING IN CONTRAST: A CONTEMPORARY KITCHEN IN THE PRESERVED DERELICTION.

This is certainly not the solution for everybody,
but it is visually stunning and original.

Manor Farm

ARCHITECT: TRANSITION BY DESIGN

LOCATION: BOARS HILL, OXFORD

BUDGET: £200,000–£250,000

PROJECT FINISHED: 2017

◀

4.11 THE HOUSE,
SEEN FROM THE
FORMAL GARDEN,
WITH THE
EXTENSION TO THE
LEFT.

If you are going to design an eco-extension and an upgrade of a house for an eco-blogger with some impressive credentials, then you had better know what you are doing. Fortunately, Transition by Design did when working for Natasha Ginks, who runs Renovate Green, a blog about sustainable retrofit and design for older houses.[1]

She and her husband had bought an old house in Oxfordshire and 'vowed to bring it to modern levels of comfort but not at the expense of the planet'.

Ginks is not just an enthusiast – she has an MSc in Climate Change and Sustainability and through the course of the project has become a qualified Retrofit Coordinator under PAS 2035 – the government standard to deliver sustainable energy refurbishment projects in domestic buildings.

Ginks and her husband started renovating the house themselves, but when they decided they needed an extension, they started looking for an architect. As Ginks wrote on her blog, 'After six months of searching, we finally find an architect who can meet our brief for a super low-energy, low-carbon extension that works alongside the old house. Enter Transition by Design.'

The purpose of the extension was to create a new entrance sequence to the house, which would include a new kitchen, dining room, garden room and utility spaces. The architect put this at right angles to the main building, with a linking section at 45 degrees. The glazed walls provide a visual link between the formal front garden and the kitchen garden.

Holistically, the Georgian house and extension are now operating at near zero carbon.

Built in reclaimed brick and oak, the extension has a very slender roof of stressed skin panels, chosen deliberately to confound a popular belief that environmentally responsible buildings have a heavy, clunky appearance. Along with the reclaimed brick and the timber, the extension uses lime plaster, employing a set of natural materials to complement the Grade II listed original building.

The architect explained, 'A local joinery company designed and built the doors and curtain glazing. This offered good cost savings but presented problems in performance for a project designed well in excess of building regulations.'

Because the curtain walling was ordered late, some of the airtightness testing that should have been carried out at an earlier stage could not be done. These complications, plus the form of the building, meant that the very high airtightness standards for which client and architect were aiming were missed. Nevertheless, said the architect, 'Holistically, the Georgian house and extension are now operating at near zero carbon, with high levels of thermal comfort.'

And the architect had some pointers for others embarking on a project with high environmental aspirations. 'Be thorough in checking the ecological credentials of your architect. Nearly all practices now feel obliged to offer this service without necessarily having the experience or expertise.

Ecological construction is a growth market but there is a gap in the supply chain. This can mean finding the right contractor can take longer.

'Airtightness is a key and quantitative factor to assess a contractor's ability in low-energy design. We recommend asking for a certificate of their best performance as part of the tender process.'

4.12 TRANSITION BY DESIGN DELIBERATELY MADE THE ROOF SLENDER TO COUNTER PREJUDICES ABOUT SUSTAINABLE DESIGN.

4.13 THE WORK INCLUDES A NEW KITCHEN.

4.14 THE EXTENSION FORMS A LINK BETWEEN FRONT AND BACK GARDENS.

4.15 RECLAIMED BRICKS ON THE FLOOR ARE JUST ONE OF THE NATURAL MATERIALS USED.

Princes Road

ARCHITECT: HESKETH HAYDEN

LOCATION: STOCKPORT

BUDGET: £120,000

PROJECT FINISHED: 2019

4.16
UNSYMPATHETIC
ADDITIONS TO THE
REAR AND SIDE
SPOILT THE LOOK
OF THE HOUSE.

4.17 THE FINISHED
BUILDING IS LARGER,
MORE USABLE AND
DEFINITELY BETTER
LOOKING.

Some projects are simply about improving an original build and possibly adding more space to suit modern requirements. But in many cases, there is also an impetus to remove and replace unsympathetic additions from the past.

This was the case with this Victorian semidetached house in the Heaton Moor conservation area of Stockport, Greater Manchester. It was originally a handsome property but the rear had been spoilt with unsympathetic additions which included a faux-Victorian conservatory and a garage stuck on the side.

The clients wanted what so many do – more generous space, more open areas rather than small rooms, and a better connection to the garden. Architect Hesketh Hayden has given them this, working hard to satisfy their particular needs.

The architect explained, 'The concept evolved naturally from the clients' aspirations and the orientation of the house and garden; these fed directly into the brief as sketch ideas were generated and shared. The design developed collaboratively with sketches and cardboard models that helped describe the spatial intent and the relationship with existing spaces.'

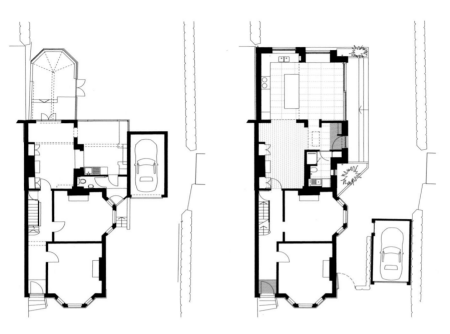

4.18 BEFORE AND AFTER PLANS OF THE GROUND FLOOR SHOWING RADICAL CHANGES, PARTICULARLY TO THE REAR OF THE BUILDING. NOTE THE NEW POSITION OF THE GARAGE.

4.19 THE WINDOW SEAT IN THE KITCHEN AND DINING AREA PROVIDES ANOTHER LINK TO THE GARDEN.

The clients were highly involved with the design process.

Good projects usually have good clients and this was the case here. The clients were highly involved with the design process, researching, taking up references and then assembling the design team and the construction team.

This was a very practical design. It needed to be comfortable, in part by improving the airtightness, and robust enough to cope with three young boys in the family. The new kitchen and dining area includes a window seat for gazing into the garden. There is a split form, with a monopitch roof on the right, looking from the garden, and a flat roof on the left. This allows for both a clerestory and a rooflight to bring light into the space.

The design uses Passivhaus principles (see page 166), with triple-glazed windows and external doors, and high levels of airtightness. Construction is of a timber frame clad in brick, insulated with natural wood fibre. A new stand-alone garage has been built at the front of the garden.

And the result? The new sits harmoniously with the old, its geometry reminiscent of the way that houses have often extended in an ad hoc manner towards the garden. From the street, nothing is visible. The architect said, 'The clients are delighted with their new space, its high levels of comfort and temperature stability, improved daylight and connection to the garden.'

4.20 THE DINING AREA IS IN IMMEDIATE CONTACT WITH THE GARDEN.

Reuse
Flat

ARCHITECT: ARBOREAL ARCHITECTURE

LOCATION: LONDON

BUDGET: 130,000

PROJECT FINISHED: 2018

◀

4.21 ALL SERVICES ARE SURFACE-MOUNTED SO THEY CAN BE REMOVED AND REUSED IN FUTURE.

Look at the remodelled ground floor of this two-storey flat in a converted house in Hackney, east London, and it looks lovely but unconventional. What strikes you first is the slightly steampunk use of stainless-steel conduit, fanning across the ceiling, containing the wires to the lighting. But look again and you realise there is a pleasingly weathered patina, that although the design is evidently contemporary, there isn't a shiny newness to it.

This is because Arboreal Architecture worked with the client to reuse as much as possible. One of the architects explained, 'The client approached us looking to reorganise the ground-floor layout of the flat and at the same time improve the sustainability of the flat. Through lots of talks about the meaning of sustainability we realised that we shared common ground in our concern and dislike for the enormous amounts of waste in our contemporary consumer culture. We realised that in construction this was perhaps even worse than consumer goods. So the project became about how reducing waste could become a design driver for interesting architecture.'

As well as some reorganisation – the kitchen moved from a secondary area to become more central – the main purpose of the refurbishment was to give the ground floor a new 'lining'. This lining contains a membrane to increase airtightness and cotton insulation to improve thermal performance. The results were impressive: airtightness came down to the standard for new buildings of $5m^3/hr$ and insulation was improved from

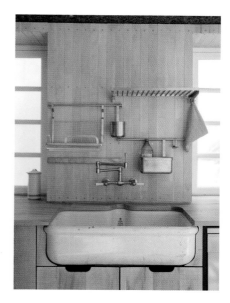

$1.1W/m^2K$ to $0.2W/m^2K$, which is 30% better than required by the building regulations for existing dwellings.

All this is important but hidden. What you can actually see in the flat are the new linings, which were made from the old wood floor of the space. They are fixed directly to the existing walls and assembled with reusable materials and fasteners (no glue) so they can be disassembled and used again in the future.

This is part of the general approach to the project. Materials are, wherever possible, reused and are in such a form that they can have another life in the future. There is a 'new' wooden floor that had a previous life as the beams of an agricultural building in Orsova, Romania.

◀

4.22 UPGRADED INSULATION SITS BEHIND THE LINING. AS MANY ITEMS AS POSSIBLE WERE REUSED.

There was a lot of 'deconstruction' involved, including taking down an internal brick wall. The broken bricks, along with waste concrete and wood, went into gabions (metal cages filled with masonry, more commonly rocks) to make a new wall in the garden. Old windows became a glazed partition in the office. The old granite worktop was repolished and reused as preparation surfaces in the new kitchen. Remaining materials were audited and recycled by a local waste contractor. The rather steampunk conduits for lighting were the result of a decision to surface-mount all services so they could be removed or replaced easily.

Because of the desire to minimise waste, Arboreal Architecture audited everything carefully. They said in a statement, '20m³ of "waste" arose from the deconstruction phase (the equivalent of 250 bin bags) but through innovative design we were able to find a new use for 43% of it directly on site. The remaining material left the site and, with a carefully selected recycling company, all but three bin bags were recycled.

'In construction we sourced 22% of our materials from the existing site ... A further 57% of materials were specified from reused sources such as the cotton insulation from jeans deposited in French clothes banks.'[2]

In future, Arboreal Architecture say that 89% of the materials could be directly reused elsewhere, 10% could be recycled and only 1% would contribute to future waste.

None of this would be as valuable if this were not also a beautiful, liveable project. For anybody contemplating a similar project,

The project became about how reducing waste could become a design driver for interesting architecture.

Arboreal Architecture advise, 'Make some time to be hands-on with the process so that you can see the materials and finishes that are possible with the reclaimed materials. They won't be as predictable or available to review so early in the design process as new-bought products. You may need a bit of extra patience and flexibility for this process. The unknowns of working with reclaimed materials are a bit like Christmas; sometimes there are wonderful surprises and other times you don't get quite what you want.'

4.23 BRICK RUBBLE FROM A DEMOLISHED INTERNAL WALL HAS GONE INTO GABIONS TO FORM A NEW WALL IN THE GARDEN.

➤
4.24 GREAT
THOUGHT HAS
GONE INTO EVERY
ELEMENT TO
ENSURE THIS IS A
WELCOMING PLACE
TO LIVE.

➤
4.25 UNLIKE
MANY SHINY
NEW PROJECTS,
THERE IS A PATINA
FROM THE REUSE
OF MATERIALS
THAT IS VERY
ATTRACTIVE.

Terraced House

ARCHITECT: COWPER GRIFFITH ARCHITECTS

LOCATION: CAMBRIDGE

BUDGET: HOUSE: £270,000 **ANNEXE:** £206,000

PROJECT FINISHED: 2016

COLMAN'S STARCH

◄

4.26 THE REBUILT
OUTBUILDING
NOW HOUSES
ACCOMMODATION
FOR VISITORS, PLUS
A GALLERY/STUDIO
SPACE.

➤

4.27 THE KITCHEN IN
THE REFURBISHED
MAIN HOUSE.

➤

4.28 THE NEW
FRONTAGE
REFERENCES THE
SHOP THAT WAS
ONCE THERE.

If you buy a house that has been converted into bedsits and want to turn it back into a family home, you know there will be a lot of work to do. The clients of this terraced house in Cambridge, however, wanted to do more than just knock out the extra kitchen facilities and update the décor (magenta ceilings, anyone?). And they had a more complex than usual building to deal with. The house was an end-of-terrace in a conservation area and also had a disused stable block behind it, with first-floor storage above, and a small courtyard garden that was partially covered by a lean-to roof.

The clients found Cowper Griffith on personal recommendation from a friend who had employed the practice. In fact, it turned out that the project architect lived only a few doors away, so this really was a local project.

The brief was to open up the house to improve the light and views, and to return it to a single residence with guest accommodation in the disused outbuilding. The clients also wanted to create a courtyard garden.

In addition to the functional changes, they wanted to improve the thermal performance, switching to renewable energy wherever possible. And they wanted the outbuilding to have a wheelchair-accessible bathroom and bedroom.

On a more whimsical note, the owners discovered that the house had once been a corner shop and decided to restore the frontage to look like a shop front, although the entrance to the house remains round the corner.

There were a number of changes made to the main house, including replacing the single-storey rear extension with a new one with an insulated cavity wall. This now has direct access to the rear courtyard garden. A parapet wall conceals a flat roof that can be reached from the second bedroom, and acts as an extension of the garden.

In order to bring in more light, two conservation rooflights (designed to look appropriate on older buildings) were installed above the attic rooms. A sun tunnel brings light into one of the bathrooms that would otherwise have been very dark.

Two solar-thermal panels on the south-facing section of the roof help to heat hot water for the house.

An old lean-to passageway has been replaced with a glazed enclosure. It sits against a boundary wall which has been rebuilt as a cavity wall. There is a standing-seam zinc roof with three rooflights.

The most radical work, however, was done on the outbuildings, or rather the wreck of the outbuildings. What is there now is a new building on the footprint of the old. However, it uses the original bricks in the insulated cavity walls. The upper storey is timber. A staircase provides access to a first-floor gallery/studio space. The intention was to retain the existing scale and character of the outbuilding using a similar range of materials while creating a thermally efficient living space.

4.29 THERE ARE THREE ROOFLIGHTS IN THE REBUILT LINK BUILDING.

4.30 THE GUEST
BEDROOM IN THE
ENTIRELY REBUILT
ANNEXE. ONE OF THE
STIPULATIONS WAS
THAT THERE SHOULD
BE A WHEELCHAIR-
ACCESSIBLE
BEDROOM.

The most radical work was done
on the outbuildings.

connecting
to outside

5

One thing the Covid-19 pandemic has taught many of us is how much we value the outdoors, and a connection to growing things and recreational space. Not everybody is fortunate enough to have a garden, but for those who are, it seems ridiculous not to make the most use of it. A garden should be easy to reach and, on colder days, we should be able to look out over it.

Yet it is surprising how many homes do not address their gardens well. There may be only a small door and a meagre window looking into the garden. Sometimes there is not a direct route at all. Somebody I know had to reach her garden through her bathroom and although that is extreme it is an indication of how ill thought-out some houses are. Often ad hoc extensions have made matters worse. Narrow extensions tacked onto the back of houses can be dark and act more as a blockage than as access.

The clients of the homes in this section all wanted better access to their gardens. They wanted to be able to get out there easily, they wanted to be able to look out on the garden, and possibly, if they were fortunate, to the view beyond. And they also wanted to look back from the garden to the house and see something attractive. Sometimes they may want to eat in the garden. At other times, when the weather is inclement, they may want to eat indoors but looking out. Opening up the space allows this to be possible, to have a feeling of being in the garden while under cover.

In some cases, clients have generous gardens and are happy to occupy a substantial area with an extension. Others, on more modest plots, will want to be very careful how much land they grab. Some of the projects shown here have a deliberately small footprint, yet have an impact on the house out of all proportion to their size.

Just one word of warning. While in many ways it is desirable to blur the line between inside and outside, in one sense one needs a clear distinction. That is in terms of energy efficiency and thermal comfort. There it must be clear where the barrier is. Shading and insulation are essential. In the past there have been too many ill-considered stick-on conservatories that guzzle energy in the winter and roast users in the summer. We do not want to make those mistakes again. A good architect should, of course, prevent them.

◄

5.1 SYCAMORE HALL BY PAUL TESTA ARCHITECTURE, SEE PAGE 118.

Sycamore Hall

ARCHITECT: PAUL TESTA ARCHITECTURE

LOCATION: BOLSTERSTONE, SHEFFIELD

BUDGET: £170,000

PROJECT FINISHED: 2017

◄

5.2 NOW WITH TWO
SMALL EXTENSIONS,
THE BUNGALOW IS
IN A MAGNIFICENT
SETTING.

Look at the before photos of this bungalow in Bolsterstone, to the northwest of Sheffield, and you may wonder why anybody – or at least anybody with an aesthetic sensibility – would buy it. But then look outside and the views are stunning. They, alone, would be a reason for living there. And in fact, as the transformation shows, this was a building with plenty of potential.

The clients, John and Jean Bloxam, chose it as their retirement home and they wanted it to be 'future-proofed' – filled with light, warm and easy to live in. The bungalow did have a small lower-ground floor, which included a third bedroom. The architect created two small extensions and placed rooflights carefully to bring in the light the clients craved.

Three special windows were created to frame the views, two with window seats so the owners can actually 'sit in' the view. These window seats are lined with timber, a high-quality material that has been used in special places in relatively small quantities, since the budget was limited. In general, materials are simple and inexpensive.

►

5.3 A BUILDING WITH
POTENTIAL – THIS IS
WHAT THE INTERIOR
LOOKED LIKE
WHEN THE CLIENTS
BOUGHT IT.

The transformation shows that this was a building with plenty of potential.

5.4 THE CLIENTS WANTED A HOME THAT WAS WARM, LIGHT AND EASY TO LIVE IN – AND THEY HAVE REALISED THEIR DREAM.

5.5 LOOKING TOWARDS THE MASTER BEDROOM – THE ADDITION OF ROOFLIGHTS HAS MADE AN ENORMOUS DIFFERENCE.

An important part of the project was improving the thermal behaviour of the building. Retrofitting of internal wall insulation, the installation of triple-glazed windows, airtightness work and mechanical ventilation have made the bungalow a warm and quiet place to live in. The project was designed using the Passivhaus Planning Package (a tool for creating extremely energy-efficient homes) to achieve an energy consumption of 48 kWh/m^2 per year.

The architect said, 'We supported John and Jean throughout their project, from planning right through to construction. We helped them to choose the right contractor, manage their costs and worked with their contractor to deliver this fantastic project to a very high standard.'

And the clients' view? They said, 'Much of the good design is summed up in the living room main window and box seat – economically enlarging an existing window space, and transforming it into one of the centrepieces of the building, both visually and functionally. Young and old are drawn to it, they love it.'

Charred
House

ARCHITECT: RIDER STIRLAND ARCHITECTS

LOCATION: LONDON

BUDGET: £159,000 PLUS VAT

PROJECT FINISHED: 2020

◄

5.6 THE CHARRED-TIMBER EXTENSION PROVIDES ONLY AN ADDITIONAL 9M² OF SPACE, BUT HAS TRANSFORMED THE HOUSE.

◄

5.7 THE UNLOVELY CLOSET EXTENSION AT THE BACK OF THE HOUSE WAS DEMOLISHED AND REPLACED.

The clients for this house faced a familiar dilemma – their Victorian home, in Ladywell, southeast London, had an unlovely two-storey 'closet wing' extension at the back, which was cold and turned its back on the garden. They wanted to improve this connection, and to have an open-plan kitchen, dining and family room. But they didn't want to eat up too much of the garden doing it.

In many cases the solution would be to fill in the side return, but here the architect, Rider Stirland, took a more radical and successful approach, removing the closet wing and replacing it with a new extension that is partly two storey and partly single storey.

On the first floor, the addition became a study that offers entirely equal elements to each of the two adults living in the house – not only their own desks and shelves, but also a window for each.

On the ground floor, the kitchen, WC and utility have moved to the centre of the house, with a flexible family/dining room at the rear.

A glazed pivot door from the rear of the kitchen and an oriel window from the family room provide a strong connection to the garden. A rooflight above the external door brings in more light.

The architect has designed the form of the extension so that it sits comfortably with the neighbours. Cladding is with stock brickwork, charred-timber boards and gold-coloured flashings installed in a measured composition.

The clients, Anna and Andrew, find that because they see the garden more easily, the family is spending more time outside, playing, relaxing and planting. Life indoors is better too, as they can cook, play and eat in the same space, with the flexibility to separate off the living room as desired.

They said, 'Our favourite part of the project is the oriel window seat. The closest room to the garden used to be the utility, so you only really looked out when doing the washing! Now, on the window seat you feel like you are floating right among the flowers. It's lovely when sunny but what we didn't expect was how fun it would be in a storm. It's the perfect place to sit and watch the wind and rain batter against the glass. At night we can even look straight up and spot the local bats darting to and fro, catching their dinner!'

On the window seat you feel like you
are floating right among the flowers.

5.8 THE GARDEN LOOKS SO MUCH MORE TEMPTING NOW, AND DRAWS THE FAMILY OUT.

5.9 THE HOUSE NOW HAS A SPACIOUS KITCHEN, WITH ROOM TO EAT.

5.10 THE FEEL OF THE ENTIRE HOUSE HAS BEEN TRANSFORMED.

Thermal performance is also much better, which became particularly noticeable when both parents were working in the first-floor study during lockdown.

This was also a highly affordable project, with a net construction cost below £1,750/m². And despite the fact that the project has made such a difference to the house and its owners, the net additional space is just 9m², meaning that as much of the garden as possible has been preserved.

Grove Park

ARCHITECT: O'SULLIVAN SKOUFOGLOU ARCHITECTS
LOCATION: LONDON
BUDGET: £125,000
PROJECT FINISHED: 2020

◄

5.11 BEAUTIFUL ASH
JOINERY CREATES
AN ELEGANT,
SPACIOUS FEEL.

▶

5.12 WHAT A
CONTRAST WITH
THE PREVIOUS
RATHER DARK,
DEPRESSING SPACE,
SHOWN IN THIS
PHOTOGRAPH.

There is a great advantage when a client knows what they want in a fundamental sense – in other words, how they want their home to work. And the owner of this three-storey 1980s red-brick house in southeast London did. The house had been built with an integral garage, which she didn't need. She also wanted a single space on the ground floor, forming a bridge between the formal garden at the front and the deliberately wilder garden at the back. The kitchen needed to be at the heart of the space, with the dining area facing the street. Not surprisingly, she wanted more light.

By taking out the garage, the architect was able to give the client the additional space she wanted, without needing an extension, which would have blown the budget. The exact arrangement was determined by the structural solution – the additional structure that was needed to hold up the floors above, when the internal walls had been removed.

The solution here was a single exposed ash flitched beam (a flitched beam combines timber with steel to make it stronger) running from the front to the back of the house. Shorter beams running from side to side intersect this at a number of locations. These positions dictated the position of the new apertures and moveable partitions, and where the furniture goes.

A new window on the side wall of the house brings in more light and a window seat provides a place to enjoy it. Ash, used for external doors, for window frames and for panels, dominates the space.

▲
5.13 THIS IS HOW
THE BACK OF THE
HOUSE LOOKED
PREVIOUSLY.

The architect worked closely with the maker, who prefabricated all the elements off-site, making the building process faster and less disruptive. The remaining pieces and the furniture were made in situ. The architect sourced ash-veneer plywood panels locally to match the solid material.

The architect's main concern in terms of sticking to the budget was due to some hardly visible subsidence of the flank wall, which could have been caused by the roots of trees from the nearby forest. Fortunately, it turned out to have been caused by a leaking rainwater pipe buried in the foundations, and so was relatively easy to remedy.

The architect commented on the project, 'There was a deep sense of collaboration with the client from the outset. As someone who has worked in the arts for decades, she was very keen to give us the freedom of our creative voice, within the parameters of her brief.'

There was a deep sense of collaboration with the client from the outset.

5.14 THE REAR OF THE HOUSE, WITH THE GENEROUS WINDOWS AND NEW PAVING.

5.15 THE PROJECT INCLUDED A NEW BATHROOM.

Highbury House Extension

ARCHITECT: ARCHITECTURE FOR LONDON
LOCATION: LONDON
BUDGET: £250,000
PROJECT FINISHED: 2014

5.16 THE KITCHEN, WITH ITS POLISHED CONCRETE FLOOR, HAS BEEN DUG DOWN TO THE LEVEL OF THE SMALL GARDEN.

5.17 THE FULLY OPENING GLAZING INVITES YOU TO STEP OUT INTO THE GARDEN, WHICH REALLY DOES FEEL LIKE AN OUTDOOR ROOM.

Often people talk about a garden as an outside room, but it rarely feels as much the case as in this extension of a Victorian house in Highbury, north London. You step out from the modern kitchen, with its polished concrete floor, onto a space of similar width, enclosed with a custom-made fence. This generous feel is very different to the narrow corridor that was there previously, which made it impossible to carry large objects through to the kitchen. In addition, the low ceiling height of less than 2m made the old kitchen feel oppressive.

The client asked for an improved link to the garden, and for a kitchen they could also use as a social space. The architect achieved this by demolishing an existing

conservatory and rear extension. By digging the new kitchen down to the level of the garden and also raising the ceiling, the architect has achieved a space that is virtually double the height of a standard room.

The rear part of the kitchen has a rooflight across part of its width, bringing light into the space, and the rest is occupied by a striking chandelier in which the lights reflect off a large wavy stainless-steel surface. Beyond this area, moving towards the door, the ceiling has a curved plaster profile, leading the eye towards the full-height 3.1m framed glass doors – and thence to the garden, with its limestone planters.

Talk about a transformation!

The client asked for an improved link to the garden, and for a kitchen they could also use as a social space.

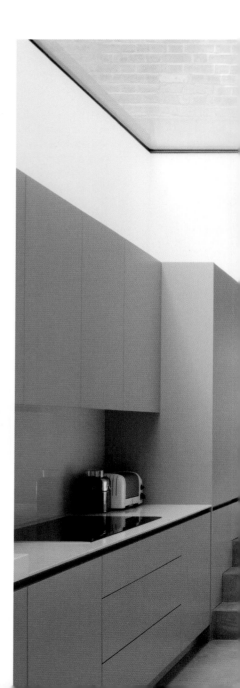

5.18 LIGHT PLAYS ON THE CHANDELIER IN AN INTRIGUING MANNER, WHICH MAKES IT MUCH MORE THAN JUST A LIGHTING ELEMENT OR A SCULPTURAL FORM.

5.19 THE FRONT PART OF THE HOUSE, THOUGH LARGELY UNCHANGED, FEELS LIGHTER AND MORE SPACIOUS THANKS TO THE NEW KITCHEN EXTENSION.

5.20 A ROOFLIGHT STRETCHES ACROSS NEARLY HALF THE WIDTH OF THE KITCHEN.

Mies X King George

ARCHITECT: CAN

LOCATION: LONDON

BUDGET: £100,000

PROJECT FINISHED: 2018

How much difference can replacing a conservatory in a building make? In the case of this listed Georgian townhouse in Highbury, north London, the answer is: a lot.

Architect CAN designed this glasshouse, replacing a poorly insulated existing extension. The original had become a storage room and acted as a barrier between the house and garden. Its replacement is, says the architect, 'a reimagined Georgian glasshouse'.

The chamfered glazed enclosure hangs from a black steel frame which serves as both structure and ornament. Although it feels like a substantial area, it occupies only the 12m² footprint of its predecessor.

From inside, the building is filled with light, but it is far from the standard glass box that has become the cliché of extensions. The external steel frame is made from the smallest I-beams that were available off the shelf, and has five repeating bays. It entirely supports the glazing, so there is no internal structure.

◄
5.21 CAN DESCRIBE THE STRUCTURE AS A REIMAGINED GEORGIAN GLASSHOUSE.
NOTE THE WAY THE CHAMFERED DOOR SLIDES INTO A POCKET IN THE BRICK WALL.

◄
5.22 THE I-BEAMS RETURN UPWARDS, CREATING DECORATIVE FINIALS.

Cleverly, the frame also serves as an ornamental element, with the I-beams returning upwards, creating finials. Solid base panels complete the external metalwork, which is black to match the original ironwork of the house.

A glazed chamfered door slides into a concealed pocket leading onto a raised patio. The external basement staircase has been moved to further improve the connection to the garden.

According to the architect, 'The project has transformed the way the clients use the house, providing them with a ground-floor living space that is well connected to the garden come rain or shine. We believe the innovative design approach adds, in some small part, to the conversation about how to respond to London's historic building fabric.

'To anyone thinking of doing work to their house, I would stress that, as with this project, additional floor area isn't always the most important factor, it's how you use the space to connect the house together and make it work for the way you live.'

5.23 THE ARCHITECT
HAS CREATED A
DELIGHTFUL GARDEN
ROOM.

5.24 ON A SUMMER'S
EVENING, THE
GLASSHOUSE ACTS
AS AN ORNAMENT
TO THE GARDEN.

Although it feels like a substantial area, it occupies
only the 12m² footprint of its predecessor.

Rugby Road Side Infill Extension

ARCHITECT: SHAPE ARCHITECTURE

LOCATION: BRIGHTON, EAST SUSSEX

COST: CONFIDENTIAL

PROJECT FINISHED: 2021

◄

5.25 THE
INCREASED WIDTH
PROVIDES A
GENEROUS SPACE
FOR COOKING AND
EATING.

This project has a relatively small side extension but, as the architect says, 'Very often a relatively small design change has a great impact and results in a far improved home.' This building was in many ways typical of homes in Brighton in that there was an underused side return and a mix of small rooms giving onto the garden but with no sense of connection between outside and inside.

By adding the side infill extension while maintaining garden access, this project opens up the interior space. A feature window merges into a rooflight with a frameless glass-to-glass connection that connects to the planted wall at the side of the property. The large-format kitchen tiles extend onto the terrace to reinforce the inside/outside feel. A green sedum roof absorbs up to 70% of the rainwater

►

5.26 ON THE LEFT-
HAND SIDE OF THE
SEDUM ROOF, YOU
CAN SEE WHERE
THE GLAZING
CONTINUES UP
FROM THE SIDE
WALL. AS WELL
AS ATTENUATING
RAINWATER, THE
GREEN ROOF
LOOKS ATTRACTIVE
FROM THE UPPER
FLOOR.

5.27 A GENEROUS ROOFLIGHT, SET BACK FROM THE GARDEN, BRINGS LIGHT INTO THE HEART OF THE HOUSE.

5.28 THE ARCHITECT
PRODUCED A
RENDERED DRAWING
WHICH HELPED
TO EXPLAIN THE
PROJECT.

that falls on it. The design process included
a variety of sketches and 3D computer
models to ensure ideas could be explored
and explained very clearly. The architect
also brought in a kitchen designer to
develop the kitchen design they had
worked up with the client.

Client Marco Presutto said, 'The end result
has just been fantastic. The best way to go
forward with a project like this is to have an
architect. We invited Jason, the architect
from Shape Architecture, into our house.
We had a chat with him, we wanted to get an
idea of what he was like. He opened us up to
other ideas, to what can and can't be done.'

5.29 THE GLAZING
SITS CLOSE TO A
LUSHLY PLANTED
WALL.

By adding the side
infill extension while
maintaining garden
access, this project
opens up the interior
space.

Hampstead House

ARCHITECT: DOMINIC MCKENZIE ARCHITECTS

LOCATION: LONDON

COST: CONFIDENTIAL

PROJECT FINISHED: 2020

5.30 THE
EXTENSION, ON
TWO FLOORS, IS
CLAD IN BRONZE
TILES.

A good architect will interpret a client's brief to give them everything they want and, ideally, more. That brief is essential. With the extension of a large Victorian house in Hampstead, northwest London, Dominic McKenzie Architects received a near-perfect brief.

The client said they wanted 'a beautifully restored period house which has been moved in to by a cool Scandinavian family in the 1950s'. They also had some specific requirements, but this sense of how they wanted their home to feel was fantastically valuable.

The architect has replaced an existing, slightly insensitive brick extension with something very different, an extension clad in bronze tiles which, with its pitched roofs, is intended to reflect the triangular gable ends of the main house and of its neighbours. Also restored are many of the original Victorian features, which were concealed or disguised in what the architect described as 'a kind of bland modernism that pleased nobody'.

There were some amendments to the original design. The planners asked the architect to reduce the length of the extension as it went beyond the end of the house. Making this change was quite complex as the architect had to avoid the repositioned pitched roofs clashing with the windows of the existing house behind.

At ground-floor level, continuous glazing in the dining room and living area allows uninterrupted views of the rear garden. Although this is much more than just a garden room, there is a real sense of being in touch with the outside. This is emphasised by the use of maple to clad the walls and ceiling of both the ground-floor and first-floor extensions.

There is a real sense of being in touch with the outside.

5.31 THE REAR OF
THE HOUSE NOW
OPENS UP TO THE
GARDEN. NOTE
THE PEAKS AND
TROUGHS OF THE
CEILING.

◄

5.32 WORK ON THE ORIGINAL HOUSE INCLUDES THE CREATION OF A WALNUT-LINED LIBRARY (SEEN THROUGH THE DOORWAY) AND RESTORATION OF ELEMENTS SUCH AS CORNICES AND ARCHITRAVES.

►

5.33 A GLASS-ROOFED PASSAGE PROVIDES A NEW ROUTE TO THE GARDEN.

►►

5.34 ON THE FIRST FLOOR, A NEW STUDY IS FILLED WITH LIGHT AND HAS TREMENDOUS VIEWS.

The dining-room ceiling follows the peaks of the roof, lifting up and therefore giving an additional feeling of space.

The bronze tiles that clad the extension are unfinished and will weather gradually over time. Intended as a complement to the brickwork, they are handmade with a slight irregularity, which brings a crafted feeling to the extension.

At the side of the house there is a new glass-roofed passage that links to the extension and provides a new way through to the garden.

With a project like this, which makes a significant addition to an existing house, success depends as much on what is done with the original building as with the new. Here, there has been extensive restoration. Previous owners had removed an original staircase leading from the basement to the second floor, and the architect reinstated a historically accurate new one. New doors, cornices, architraves, skirtings and ceiling roses are as historically accurate as possible.

Interior designer Suzy Hoodless worked on the interiors, which include a walnut-lined library and workspace which opens off the main living room. The library has an inset fireplace lined with Welsh slate. The kitchen is in pale grey with a matching grey marble island and splashback. The master bathroom is lined with travertine.

The end result is a house that works well as a whole, but with elements that clearly come from different periods – just the place for a cool Scandinavian family of the 1950s.

Hive
House

ARCHITECT: NIMTIM ARCHITECTS

LOCATION: LONDON

BUDGET: £75,000

PROJECT FINISHED: 2017

This project, in Lewisham, southeast London, was definitely an example of a client wanting to get as much benefit as possible for a limited budget. In this case, they spent just £75,000 on the project, completed in 2017. For this they got a space that the Edwardian terrace house had not previously offered – somewhere large enough for the whole family to engage in different activities.

Where previously there had been an unimpressive small conservatory-type extension to one side of the rear, and a cramped kitchen and utility room, now there is a generous kitchen and dining area that runs across the full width of the house, with a slightly narrower area stepping out beyond the dining area.

This change in width is enough to give a sense of different spaces, albeit part of a large space that flows between the two volumes. It makes the back of the house into somewhere deliberately designed, rather than an afterthought. And, because of this, it greatly improves the relationship between house and garden.

The client found the architects because one of the family was sharing an office with them. As one of the architects explained, 'They liked our approach, which focused on specific client needs through games and discussions to develop a brief that was tailored to their requirements.'

5.36 STACK-BONDED
BRICKWORK WITH
PATINATED LEAD
ABOVE GIVES AN
UNUSUAL FEEL
BUT MAINTAINS A
DOMESTIC SCALE.

▶

5.37 THE REAR OF THE
HOUSE PREVIOUSLY
HAD AN OUTDATED
CONSERVATORY-TYPE
EXTENSION.

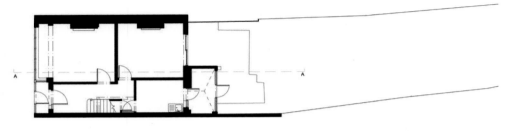

existing ground floor plan

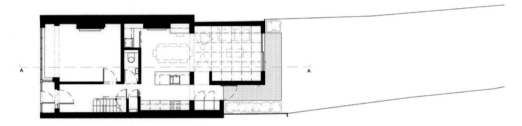

proposed ground floor plan

The structure is entirely made of timber, in a square grid of structural plywood that is exposed and, in some places, used for storage. It adds to the interest of the space. Externally, the stack-bonded brickwork with recessed mortar joints gives an unusual appearance, but one that fits with the domestic scale.

There is a focus on simplicity throughout, which was both an aesthetic choice and a strategy to keep costs down. Doors and windows have dark grey aluminium frames. The fascias above are of patinated lead over external plywood and the floor and worktops are poured concrete.

The architects said, 'Everyone contributed to the design of the house, with the family choosing colours and tiles, and the contractor finding the solution for the kitchen handles and fabricating them with his father in Poland. The project demonstrates the value of spending time on the design at the outset. There is often a temptation to try and create as much space as possible, particularly when dealing with a small house like this one. The project emerged from a more intimate and detailed understanding of the family and their daily routines and dynamics. It resulted in a project that truly reflected their characters and personalities.'

5.38 BEFORE AND AFTER PLANS DEMONSTRATE HOW LITTLE SPACE WAS ADDED AND THE CHANGE IN WIDTH THAT GIVES THE IMPRESSION OF TWO ROOMS IN ONE.

5.39 THIS IS A REAL FAMILY HOME, WITH ALL FAMILY MEMBERS INVOLVED IN THE PROCESS OF BRIEFING AND SELECTION OF ELEMENTS.

The project demonstrates the value of
spending time on the design at the outset.

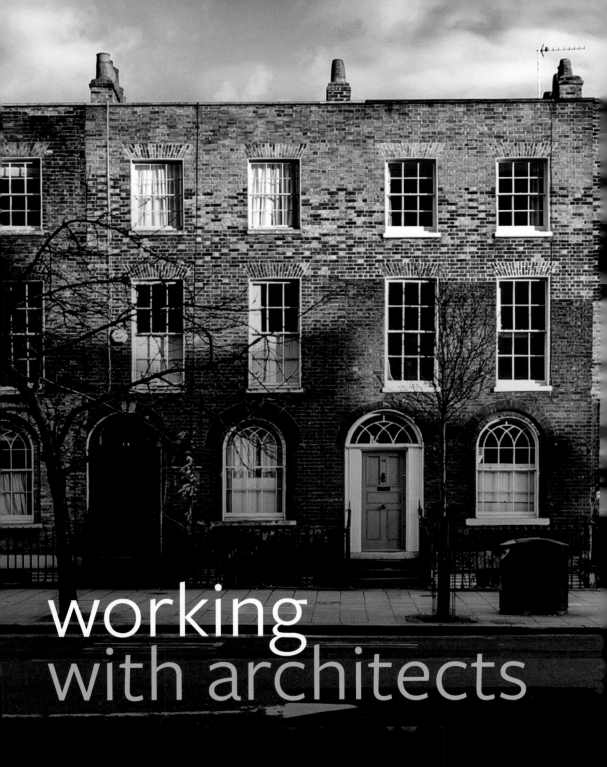

working
with architects

6

The projects in this book vary in size, type and location. They only have two things in common. They are all domestic projects, that is they are people's homes, and they have all been designed by architects. Indeed, they have all been designed by Chartered Practices, accredited by the RIBA (the Royal Institute of British Architects; see page 155 for the criteria for becoming a Chartered Practice).

What is clear is that each of these projects makes a strong argument for using an architect. They show, in each case, how the client has worked with the architect to really understand what they are looking for in terms of improving their homes. Architects are trained to think about the way that space works, to interpret the desires of their clients and to solve problems. Their extensive training and experience mean they understand planning, the intricacies of the building process, the regulations that have to be observed and the way to make a building energy efficient and sustainable.

Whether our homes date from Georgian and Victorian times, or from the 20th or even early 21st century, few of us are living in those homes in the way that was originally envisaged. Our family structures are different, our technology is different. Never mind the prevalence of smartphones and other digital devices – when some of these homes were originally designed, there was no running water or electricity. An accretion of changes may result in places that just about work – but only just.

The Covid-19 pandemic has made a lot of us think differently about our homes, as we have spent more time there. They are not just places for sleeping and relaxing, but places to work, to learn, to entertain. How much privacy do we need in a home? How much interaction do we want to encourage? How much connection do we need to the outside world? Do we have enough space? These are all problems that architects can help to solve.

Architects are trained in spatial thinking, in envisaging what could go where and how spaces can be transformed. They can, of course, think about materials: the best structures and finishes for your walls, floors, roofs and ceilings. But the most important element they can manipulate is one that is not available at the builders' merchant. It is light. Our experience of buildings during daylight hours is enormously dependent on the light within them – the quantity and quality, the angles from which it comes. Coupled with this, the views that a building can frame can add enormously to our enjoyment. Similarly, at night, the design and position of lighting can have a great impact. This is all something that a talented architect can achieve.

Take the case of one of the clients quoted on the RIBA's website. Polly from Cambridge said, 'Our space needed reimagining. Our architect transformed it.

6.1 GEORGIAN
HOUSE BY LYNCH
ARCHITECTS, SEE
PAGE 86.

The thing I love most is the sense of space and light. I would never have imagined this was possible in a tiny terraced house. There is light from room to room.'

With all these attributes, it may seem that the question is not 'Why use an architect?' but 'Why on earth wouldn't you use an architect?' There are, of course, times when you don't need an architect. As a rough rule of thumb, architects are happy to work on projects with a value of £50,000 or more. Another way of looking at this is that you should consider using an architect if you are planning a significant change – something more than replacing windows or upgrading a kitchen or bathroom, something that means the plans of the building or part of the building will look significantly different once the work is done.

There are other reasons, though, that people don't use architects, and they are generally due to misapprehension. This is a pity, as they are missing out. The reasons include:

- not understanding what an architect is
- worrying about how to choose an architect
- not understanding what an architect does
- worrying about the cost of using an architect.

If you have any of those fears, this book seeks to address them.

While every architect works in a slightly different way, there are many broad similarities in approach. When looking for an architect, and subsequently working with them, discuss their approach and make sure you understand how they like to do things. Just as there is no single correct solution to designing a building, so there is no single way of working that is the best. The following, however, should give you a good general idea of what to expect.

So what is an architect? To become an architect, it is necessary to follow a specific process of professional education and registration. Anybody who calls themselves an architect has to have completed this, as the title 'architect' is protected by law in the UK. Someone can call themselves an 'architectural designer' or a 'building designer' and, because there is no 'protection of function' in the UK, they are allowed to design buildings. Indeed, anybody at all *can* design a building. Whether or not they are qualified or sufficiently skilled to do so is another matter. Common sense (and sometimes bitter experience) dictates that it is better to use a professional who is actually qualified and regulated to design the changes to your home.

All architects complete their education over at least seven years and at the end of it they have to register with the Architects Registration Board if they want to work as an architect. Most also become members of the RIBA, which is a professional body founded for the advancement of architecture.

Membership of the RIBA is on an individual basis, but architectural practices (the term used for architectural businesses) can apply to become RIBA Chartered Practices. In order to do so, they must fulfil the following criteria:

- At least one of the full-time principals (that is a director or partner) must be a RIBA Chartered Member.

- At least one in eight of all staff must be a RIBA Chartered Member and all of the architectural work that the practice does must be supervised by a RIBA Chartered Member.

- The practice must commit to operating policies regarding best practice in: employment; equality, diversity and inclusion; health and safety; environmental management; and quality management.

In other words, a RIBA Chartered Practice is the gold standard for architectural practices, and choosing one of these would be a sensible move. These are the practices that the RIBA can recommend to you if you want help in choosing an architect.

Choosing an architect

If you choose to work with a RIBA Chartered Practice you will be working with an architect who meets professional standards and the strict criteria set by the RIBA. But that does not mean that every Chartered Practice will be right for you and your project. Since the architect will have a major influence on your home and on the way you live for years and possibly decades to come, it is essential that you make the right choice. This isn't as difficult as it sounds. Just as few of us believe there is only one perfect partner out there in the world for us, there isn't only one perfect architect for you. You want an architect who is a good fit for you, and your project.

Where should they be based?

The UK has some of the best architects in the world, and as a result they work all over the globe. But those international schemes are usually massive, and small projects are a different matter. However big your home improvements feel to you, they will be, in architectural terms, a small project. So the more local your architect is to you, the easier things are likely to be. If you live in a major city, you should be able to find an architect within that city and ideally in your part of the city (after all, it can take as long to get across

London as to traverse a couple of counties). If you live somewhere remote, you may need to compromise on this, especially as many architects cluster in cities.

If you have to compromise on distance (and you certainly shouldn't choose an architect purely because they are the only one within half an hour's travel), then you need to think about making this work for you. The architect needs to make at least one detailed visit to your home. After that, are you happy to communicate on Zoom or Teams? Are they going to manage the build process or are you happy to do that yourself? If the former, and site visits are going to be tricky for them, how will they manage this? The more you can sort out these details early on, the more harmonious your relationship should be.

How big?

The largest architects' practice in the UK is Foster + Partners, headed by Sir Norman Foster. According to the 2021 AJ100 survey run by *The Architects' Journal*, the practice employs 383 architects and a total of 1,180 staff.[1] In contrast, around 75% of RIBA-registered practices consist of 10 architects or fewer. And while Foster + Partners has done some private homes – for example, a luxurious villa in Turkey completed in 2019 – nobody would expect a practice of that size to concern itself with a kitchen extension to a Victorian semi.

So, realistically, you are going to be working with a medium or small practice – and it could be as small as a sole practitioner. There are advantages and disadvantages. A larger practice will have more resources. If an individual in the practice comes across a problem they have not met before, someone else in the practice may have experienced it. And if somebody is ill, or occupied with another job that has gone wrong, then a colleague can step in.

On the down side, with a larger practice, your job is unlikely to be the most important they are undertaking. If you choose to work with this size of practice, it will be worth

6.2 IF YOU CHOOSE TO WORK WITH A VERY NEW PRACTICE, THEY WILL PUT THEIR ALL INTO MAKING THE PROJECT SUCCEED. GAGARIN STUDIO WAS VERY YOUNG WHEN IT DESIGNED THIS REAR EXTENSION IN MARPLE BRIDGE. (SEE PAGE 27.)

establishing who exactly will be in charge of your project and ensure that you will be dealing with them throughout.

If you choose to go with a small or very small practice, the pros and cons will be different. Your job will be really important to them. They may well be a new practice, started by architects who are still at an early point in their careers or who have left bigger practices to start up on their own. They are likely to be full of enthusiasm. And they may have new ideas and a refreshingly different approach. These should help compensate for any lack of experience.

How do you choose an architect?

There are numerous ways to find an architect. Personal recommendation is probably the most common. Quite a few of the projects in this book have come about that way, with the relationship initiated by anything from being at school together to sharing an office with an architect. These projects are, by definition, successful, otherwise they would not appear here. But, of course, the first architect you meet may not be the best one for you or your project.

That concept of recommendation can spread a little wider by using neighbourhood groups to seek recommendations – local WhatsApp groups or websites such as Nextdoor. You may see a project in a magazine or an exhibition. You might even be inspired by the projects in this book! At least one of the clients in this book found their architect by attending one of the 'Don't move, improve' exhibitions hosted by New London Architecture.

It may be that you love the first architect you come across so much that you are happy to go with them. But it makes sense to speak to more than one, so you can make

6.3 THE PROJECT AT CAROLINE PLACE CAME ABOUT BECAUSE AMIN TAHA, THE FOUNDER OF GROUPWORK, WENT TO SCHOOL WITH THE CLIENT. (SEE PAGE 49.) YOU MAY NEED TO FIND YOUR ARCHITECT BY A MORE FORMAL ROUTE.

comparisons. And you may not know how to find them.

This is where the RIBA can help. Its free-to-use Find an Architect (FAA) service on architecture.com enables you to shortlist Chartered Practices that are suitable for your type of project, by submitting some basic information. Each shortlisted practice has a profile on FAA which includes past projects for you to review, together with their contact details for you to follow up – or you can send a message to the practices anonymously.

If this feels too complex and impersonal, the RIBA also runs a bespoke service called the Client Referrals service, where a member of staff will create a shortlist of practices on your behalf.

Further research

Once you have a shortlist, the first step will be to review practice information online – either on their Find an Architect profile page on architecture.com or their own website. A typical site should have a section of residential projects as a category. Have a look and see if you like what is there. You are not looking for a project that is exactly like the one you want, but an overall style that appeals to you. Don't worry if all the projects appear to be bigger than yours. There may be work of a smaller scale that they are not showing.

It will be useful if the architect has solved a problem that is similar to yours, such as working with a historic building, or creating an extra room in a flat with no garden to expand into. But if you like the work in general, don't be too prescriptive. The fact they have not yet solved a problem like yours, doesn't mean they won't be able to.

There will also probably be a section called 'about us' which will tell you about the principals in the practice. It will give you an idea of how big the practice is, which may be helpful, and where they have worked before, so you can understand more about their experience.

There may also be an element on the site called 'our approach' or 'our philosophy'. This will help you get to know their approach.

Once you have finalised your shortlist of (say) three, you need to meet them and to take up references. It's up to you in which order to do this. My personal preference would be to meet first, so you get a feeling of who you would like to work with, and then to follow up those references. This may be the more time-saving approach.

6.4 BE CLEAR ABOUT WHAT YOU WANT. THE OWNERS OF SYCAMORE HALL, IN SHEFFIELD, KNEW THEY WANTED TO IMPROVE THE VIEWS. (SEE PAGE 119.)

Meeting your architect

Contact the architect with a fairly simple message that tells them where you live, what sort of home you have and very roughly what you are looking for – for example, making the ground floor more interconnected, reshaping the whole house and garden, or creating a space to work in at home. This will give them a sense of the scale of your project. A good architect may say they are too busy to take on more work or that your project is too big or too small for them, in which case they might be able to suggest an alternative practice. Such recommendations are worth listening to.

The next stage is for each of your shortlisted architects to meet you in your home, for an initial consultation. This is a good opportunity for you to get to know each other. The only reason they might not visit your home is if you are in the process of buying a new place and don't have access to it. Even then, visiting you at your current home would be a good idea, as they can see how you live.

So, what do you do when they come? You explain what you are looking for, and give them an early version of your brief. You show them how you live and tell them your aspirations. Tell them how big your budget is, and see if they think what you are asking for is feasible. If they suggest something different, which may be more expensive, it may be worth considering. Some people can find more money if there is a good reason. But if you can't, be clear about it. Also discuss with them what you would be asking them to do. Would they be appointing a contractor and supervising the construction, or would you do that yourself, or appoint a project manager?

Also ask them if they think that any other professionals would be needed to work on your project. And, in terms of the architect, would the person you are meeting see the project all the way through, or would they pass it over to a colleague? Working with an architect can be an intense relationship, and it is good to know your day-to-day contact as well as the team you will be dealing with.

This first consultation is usually free. The architect should give you some idea about whether the project is practical/feasible and how they might approach it. Some might submit a few ideas to help the discussion and test out what you like. It is a chance to see if you are in sympathy with their ideas, and vice versa. Don't forget that design is the architect's profession and they need to be paid for their work.

The meeting is also a chance for you to discover if this is an architect with whom you could work. Are you on enough of the same wavelength to communicate effectively? Is the architect listening to your requirements? Do you understand what they are talking about? Do you feel they get you, your family and your home? Remember that this is an opportunity for the architect to decide whether they want to work with you, as well as you deciding if you want to work with them.

If you are happy with your meeting, and you think you have found 'your' architect, then, if you have not done so already, it will be time to take up references.

References

Ideally, you want to talk to a couple of clients who have used the architect before. Ask the architect if they will put you in touch. If you have already identified projects from the website that seem relevant, ask to be put in contact with those people. Ideally, you should ask both to meet the previous clients and to see the finished jobs, but this is not always possible.

Remember that building projects are complex, and there are likely to have been some problems along the way, so don't expect to hear that everything was perfect. Still, talking to people once the job is complete, they should be generally positive, although there are likely to be some caveats.

Here are some questions you may like to ask:

- How was the relationship with the architect?

- Was the architect available to answer questions when needed?

- Did the architect take the client's desires into account?

- If the architect appointed and managed the contractor, did this go well?

- How did the architect deal with difficulties in the course of the project?

- Was the project completed within the agreed budget? If not, why not? (If, for instance, unexpected problems were discovered in the existing structure or the ground, or a supplier went bust, or the client changed their minds, there may be unavoidable cost overruns.) Was the project completed on time? (The unavoidable problems that can cause a project to go over budget are likely to affect the timetable as well.) Are there any lingering problems or unfinished elements?

- If the client had another project, would they work with the same architect again?

If the answers to all these questions are largely positive, and you are enthusiastic about the conversation you had with the architect, then it is probably time to appoint your architect.

The next thing you need to do is to work on the brief. This is vital since, alongside appointing your architect, this is the most important thing you can do. It may even be more important than appointing your architect.

Developing the brief

You should be able to work with your architect on refining your brief. They should help you with further questions that you can ask, and they will see the possibilities and limitations of your existing property. In addition, they will know how they have solved similar problems in similar properties. But architects are not mind-readers. They do not understand the intricacies of your life, your hopes and your discontents as well as you do. It is therefore up to you to tell the architect what you want in terms of aspiration, but not in detail.

6.5 THE CLIENTS FOR THIS HOUSE IN HAMPSTEAD WERE VERY SPECIFIC. THEY SAID THEY WANTED 'A BEAUTIFULLY RESTORED PERIOD HOUSE WHICH HAS BEEN MOVED IN TO BY A COOL SCANDINAVIAN FAMILY IN THE 1950S'. (SEE PAGE 142.)

So, for example, it is better to say, 'I would like a kitchen where we can all eat together and where the children can do their homework,' rather than, 'I would like the kitchen to be two feet wider.' It is also worth thinking ahead. You will be embarking on a major project, and the fundamental changes to your home should suit not only the way you are living now but also the way you expect to live in five or ten years' time.

Below are some of the things that may be important to include in your brief. It is quite a long list but there are plenty of elements that an individual could ignore. For example, if you are desperate for an extra bedroom and have a limited budget, it won't take you long to realise that you don't need a home cinema.

Actual or anticipated changes to your household This may involve the birth or adoption of children; cohabitation or separation; adult children leaving home or boomeranging back; an older relative moving in; employing an au pair; getting a lodger; new pets (a gerbil may make little difference, but a couple of great Danes could).

Actual or anticipated changes in circumstances Examples include illness or disability; retirement; planning for later life; children needing their own bedrooms.

Work or study Do one or more members of your household work a significant amount from home, or intend to do so? Are they running a business from home that requires more than just a desk and computer? Is anybody in your household studying or planning to study? Are you home-schooling?

Interests and hobbies Does a member of your household enjoy an occupation that requires a lot of space of a particular type, such as painting or furniture-making? Do you want a gym or a home cinema or a sauna?

6.6 THIS JAPANESE-INSPIRED APARTMENT IN LONDON'S BARBICAN MOSTLY USES SCREENS INSTEAD OF SOLID WALLS TO DELINEATE SPACES. COULD THIS WORK FOR YOU? (SEE PAGE 162.)

Storage Is there enough storage in your present property? Is it the right kind, in the right place?

Levels of tidiness It is worth being honest with yourself about how tidy you and your family are. It is true that it is almost impossible to be tidy if you don't have enough storage, but some people are inherently neat and others are not. Some designs require clean lines and an absence of clutter. They will not be right for you if you are not naturally a tidy person.

Openness and privacy Think about whether you want everybody to be in the same space or doing different activities in different rooms. You probably want some combination of the two, and may even want to use screens to create different effects at different times.

People from outside the home Do you host a lot of overnight visitors? Do you like to give big dinners? Do your children have a lot of sleepovers?

Light and connection to outside Think about whether your house is light enough or if there are particular areas where you would appreciate having more light. If you have a garden, do you want a better connection to it? Do you want to enjoy better views?

Garden Decide how precious it is. Are you willing to lose some of it to an extension? Are there things you want to protect in it? Do you want to rethink your garden? (In which case, you may, unless looking for very simple planting, also want to work with a garden designer.)

Maintenance No building is maintenance free, but some finishes are more demanding than others. Before committing to an unsealed surface or a floor that is easily scuffed, it is wise to be honest with yourself about how much effort you are willing to put in.

The best bits What do you really love in your home and not want to change? Is it the staircase where you sometimes sit and read, or the extra-large bath or the view from the bedroom window?

Your aspirations Do you want an extra bathroom? Would you like a utility room? Do you want space for a grand piano?

The feel of your home Do you want it to be a place to relax? A place to display your collections and family photos? Somewhere smart and contemporary? In keeping with the original date of construction? Do you just want a 'nice' home, or do you want it to appear in glossy magazines and on Instagram?

Sustainability Any extension will have to be in line with new and more stringent regulations on energy efficiency, and if you are having substantial work done, then it will almost certainly make sense to upgrade the existing building as well. But these are minimum requirements. You may want to go further, to make your home as

FIGURE 6.7 THE TWO-AND-A-HALF-STOREY HOUSE WAS AN EXTREMELY INGENIOUS RESPONSE TO A PLANNING CONSTRAINT ON THE MAXIMUM HEIGHT OF ANY EXTENSION. (SEE PAGE 4.)

energy-efficient as possible or to maximise the use of renewable energy. You may care a lot about saving water, about using recycled materials or ensuring that all your materials come from sustainable sources. You need to be clear about these requirements. If they are really important to you, you will want to work with an architect who shares your views.

Likes and hates Most of the elements on this list are deliberately non-prescriptive. They are about the information you can give an architect to help them do their job better. But there is no point in them working away and coming up with an answer that you immediately reject, or where you say wistfully, 'But I would really have liked...' So tell them about your prejudices. Do you really hate green roofs? Do you adore rain showers? Do you love shutters and hate curtains? This is information that is worth sharing.

What is the architect's role?

This could seem like a simplistic question. The architect is going to design the improvements to your home, aren't they? Simple. But they may also do a number of other things.

Dealing with planning

Not all home improvements need planning permission, as changes up to a certain level fall within permitted development rights. The rules are quite complicated, and your architect should advise you. The rules become even more complex if you live in a conservation area. There are a surprising number of conservation areas, and your architect should check whether you are in one or not.

If your building is listed (and Historic England estimates there are around half a million listed buildings in England[2]) then things are even more complicated. The Planning Portal states that you will need to apply for listed building consent if 'you want to alter or extend a listed building in a manner which would affect its character as a building of special architectural or historic interest'.[3]

Your architect should be able to take you through the process of applying for planning permission, producing the relevant documents for the local authority. If the architect predicts complications, they may be able to get pre-planning advice from the planners. And, in a really awkward case, they may recommend that you employ a specialist planning consultant.

Getting planning right is essential. In the worst-case scenario, if you go ahead and build without planning permission when you need it, or if the finished form is not in line with the planning consent, you could be forced to demolish the work that has been done.

Dealing with building regulations

In addition to possibly needing planning permission, you may well need building regulations approval for the work on your home. Whereas planning permission ensures that changes to a building do not spoil an area or inconvenience neighbours, building regulations set standards for the design and construction of buildings to ensure the safety and health of people in or about those buildings. They also include requirements to ensure that fuel and power are conserved and that facilities are provided for people, including those with disabilities, to access and move around inside buildings.

A local-authority inspector or other approved inspector will visit your project at the end of the work and decide if it complies with building regulations. If it does not, then some of the work will need to be redone.

In principle, if your building project contravenes building regulations, you could be prosecuted. What is probably just as worrying for homeowners is that if your work does not comply, you will not be issued with a completion or final certificate. This could make it very difficult to sell your home.

Again, this is an area that your architect should understand. There are a number of different building regulations covering different aspects of building technology. These change fairly frequently. So unless the work to your home is of such a small scale that it is exempt from building regulations, you will need your architect to take charge of this.

Sustainability

Building regulations will require certain measures to improve sustainability on all but the simplest projects. But, as mentioned earlier, you may wish to go much further than this. Indeed, your motivation for the work may be largely to improve the thermal performance of your building.

If this is your driving force, you will probably want to work with an architect who is really committed to making your home as green as possible.

On her blog Renovate Green,[4] Natasha Ginks, who is a client for one of the projects in this book (see page 100), writes, 'If you're employing an architect then check out their "green" credentials and don't be fobbed off with the old maxim that "the building regulations are so strict nowadays that all new buildings are effectively eco". I went through a couple of rounds of architects before finding one who is genuinely "green" and not just good at "green-speak".'

Ginks recommends the following:

- Find an architect with Passivhaus certification (this means 'they are trained to design structures that minimise heat loss and take advantage of free heat gains', Ginks explains). An MSc in low-carbon building design and modelling is helpful.

- Look at their previous projects ('Find out what elements inspire them and whether these fit with your priorities,' Ginks says).

- Ask them about the type of materials they design with and whether they are familiar with techniques coming across from Europe, especially Germany and Scandinavia.

This is just one person's opinion, but she makes some good points. Passivhaus is a whole-building approach to design that ensures a building uses very little energy by combining a high level of insulation with rigorous airtightness and a mechanical ventilation system with heat recovery.

EnerPHit, which is less well known, is the equivalent of Passivhaus that is used for the retrofitting of existing properties, and so is likely to be more relevant. While still demanding, it takes account of the limitations that having an existing structure impose.

If a project is to be certified as Passivhaus or EnerPHit, it must be signed off by an independent certifier. They look at the performance of the building, not just at the design. Because airtightness is so important, the quality of construction is vital and there will be airtightness tests.

6.8 THIS PROJECT HAS REUSED
DEMOLITION WASTE TO CREATE
A WALL IN THE GARDEN. YOU
COULD DO SOMETHING SIMILAR
IF PRESERVING MATERIALS IS
IMPORTANT TO YOU. (SEE PAGE
109.)

A Passivhaus designer has been trained in the process of reaching a Passivhaus standard. They may be your architect, or the architect may work with a specialist consultant. On some projects, architect and client decide that they don't actually want to go through the certification process, but that working towards it has been valuable and has improved the quality of the work.

Passivhaus is all about energy use. There are other elements of sustainability which are also important. You can talk about the use of renewable energy, such as photovoltaic panels or solar thermal panels. You may decide to opt for an all-electric house, as the renewable component of electricity is increasing.

You may be most concerned about the embodied energy in the products you are using (the energy that has gone into making them and delivering them). This will lead you to look not only at what you are using, but also at how far it has travelled – the heavier the material, the more local it needs to be.

It may be that you want to eliminate plastics as far as possible, or to use renewable materials. You may be concerned about the air quality in your home and determined to eliminate volatile organic compounds (VOCs). Reusing demolition waste may be important to you, or you may want as much vegetation as possible, inside and out. And, of course, you may want to do all these things.

Whatever your concerns, discuss these when selecting your architect, and then go into more detail with them once you embark on the project. Sustainability shouldn't be an add-on, but something you think about from the beginning.

Managing the build

You will need to appoint a contractor, or a number of contractors. At this point, the architect can bow out and leave you to manage the rest of the project yourself. You can appoint a main contractor to do the job, and they in turn can select any subcontractors, or you can appoint a number of individual contractors and manage the coordination yourself.

If you take the latter route, you will find yourself involved in a lot of work. You will have to make sure the interfaces between different trades are all covered, and juggle when somebody is delayed, or a product is not available. You may have to deal with suppliers going out of business. You will have to inspect all the work on site.

It may be simpler just to go with one main contractor, and allow them to bring in all the other trades. But on a complex project, you are putting a lot of faith in a single person or organisation. When your builder tells you that it would be simpler to do things a different way, and save time or money, you may find it difficult to make the right decision because you will not feel qualified to do so. However decent and responsible the contractor is, you need to remember that their interest is in making as large a profit as possible, and in finishing the job as quickly as possible. This does not mean they will do a bad job, but there will always be a temptation to cut corners.

Running the job yourself is, of course, feasible, and some clients have the confidence and, crucially, the time to do it. But you may not be one of those people. One option would be to employ a project manager to take on this responsibility. If, however, you are tempted to do this, why not think about using as your project manager the person who understands the project better than anybody – the architect who designed it?

If you retain the architect in this way, they will be able to help with the appointment of contractors and subcontractors as well as suppliers, consulting with you along the way.

It is also important to remember that the contractor needs a detailed document to price, if you are going to get an accurate understanding of the final price. The architect can help you draw this up.

Working with other professionals

Architects have a broad education, an understanding of what is involved in designing and making a building and great skills of coordination. They also know the limits of their knowledge. In some projects, an architect will be able to work as the sole professional, but there are many occasions when they will need to bring in other skills.

Structural engineering

Depending on the complexity of the project, you may well need to work with a structural engineer. Their involvement may range from a simple calculation of the size of beam that is needed to replace an internal wall, to the complex work involved in designing a basement (if this is really difficult, they may also call on a geotechnical engineer).

Party wall surveyor

If you live in a terraced or semidetached house you will have at least one party wall – a wall shared with another owner's property. Depending on how much structural work is involved, you may need a party wall agreement. The point of this is to specify who will be responsible for any damage that the works you carry out cause to the neighbouring property. A party wall surveyor will be responsible for drawing up this agreement and also for monitoring it (you may also have to pay for your neighbour to employ an independent party wall surveyor).

6.9 IT IS OBVIOUS THAT A COMPLEX PROJECT LIKE THIS (SEE PAGE 36) WILL NEED AN ARCHITECT, BUT SIMPLE PROJECTS WILL ALSO BENEFIT FROM ARCHITECTURAL THINKING.

Other specialists

And there could be others – a building services engineer, a Passivhaus specialist, an interior designer, a garden designer or a quantity surveyor (somebody who specialises in costs). Talk to your architect and see if any of these specialists will help to make your project the best that it can be.

Working with your architect

We have talked about the initial contacts and the briefing of your architect, but this is a relationship that will last throughout your project, and possibly beyond. You are going to need a lot of give and take. What is sometimes called a 'robust discussion' may serve you well.

Early in the project, if the architect shows you some ideas and they do not work for you, do not be polite and nod. This is the point when you can talk about what you like and don't like and, ideally, why. The longer the project goes on, the more difficult it will be to make changes, especially fundamental ones. In particular, any fundamental changes made once construction begins will be expensive and set back progress on the project.

You should not be changing the brief at this stage, but discussing how it is interpreted. And while it is important to make your views known, you should also listen to the advice the architect gives you.

How you work with your particular architect will depend on both your personality and the approach of the architect.

Presenting ideas

The output from architects' design work is typically in the form of plans (drawings of the layout of the floor) and sections (vertical slices through the buildings). Some people find these easy to read, but many who have not had the appropriate specialist training do not. While these technical drawings will be generated automatically from the design packages that architects use, there is much more they can do to get their ideas across. Some of these will help you, and may also be needed for planning applications.

These include visualisations and rendered drawings which will look much more like the finished home. Three-dimensional rendered drawings (three-dimensional drawings to which colour and texture have been added to make them look more realistic), in particular, can give a really revealing impression of the exterior.

6.10 A THREE-DIMENSIONAL RENDER LIKE THIS CAN HELP TO MAKE THE PROJECT EASIER TO UNDERSTAND. (SEE PAGE 138.)

Models, which can be anything from a simply made cardboard model up to a highly sophisticated creation by a skilled model-maker, are another way of communicating ideas.

And, if the architect wants to be really fancy, they could create a virtual-reality model, and allow you to put on goggles and walk through your home before it has even been built.

Whether or not the architect provides sophisticated tools to represent your building, it is vital that you understand what is being proposed and can discuss it.

Choosing materials

However good the representation of your project is, nothing beats seeing the actual materials. Suppliers are usually happy to let you have samples, but these present two problems. It is difficult sometimes to envisage what something will look like at scale and this is exacerbated when the material has a natural variation. Think, for example, of a highly figured piece of marble, for which a small sample will scarcely represent reality.

Travelling to see large samples, or even looking at products in use on buildings, is worthwhile. Your architect should be able to help with this.

In addition, they will probably have a good list of suppliers who they know and, if needed, can find craftspeople who can make things specially.

What about the cost?

One of the most worrying things about any building project is thinking about how much it will cost. Even extremely rich people rarely have unlimited budgets and, for most of us, there is a definite ceiling on what we can afford to spend.

There are two questions you may be asking. Can you afford an architect? And can you afford the entire project?

What does an architect charge?

An architect is a professional and will charge you for their time. Some will charge a percentage of the value of the project, so that at the beginning when you first appoint them you can agree both how much you think the project will cost, and what the architect's fee will be. This will then be charged in staged payments as the job progresses.

In the past, there were set scales for architects' fees, but the RIBA abolished the mandatory fees in 1982 and recommended fees in 1992. It is therefore up to the architect with whom you are working to fix the fees – and for you to agree them. In general, the smaller the project and the more complex it is, the higher percentage fee an architect will charge.

There are other possible ways for an architect to charge, either as a lump sum or fixed fee for each stage of the project or an hourly time charge. Charging by time gives the client very little certainty of what they will be paying.

If you do not want the architect to take on the whole project but only to take it up to planning approval stage, or only up to detailed drawings, then they should be happy to agree a lower fee.

It is important that you agree the architect's fee at the start of the project, and have a proper contract. The RIBA Domestic Building Contract is suitable for all types of projects on a client's home. Typically, if you agree a fee early on, based on the anticipated cost of the project, that should only vary if the cost of the project goes up by more than 10%. The other time when an architect may require an additional fee is if you make significant late changes to your project, deciding, after detailed design has been done, that you want to largely tear it up and start again. In effect, you will be asking them to design your home twice – and paying for it.

As to whether you can afford to have an architect – can you afford not to? You will be paying the architect for their expertise and design of your most valuable asset. Most architects charge reasonable rates, so you will not be paying an exorbitant amount.

If you choose not to use an architect but work, for example, with somebody who offers you a turnkey price for the entire design-and-build package, then you will be doing one of two things: you will either be paying for the design work in a way that is not immediately obvious to you (i.e. the cost of the design work will be incorporated in the price you are paying) or you will not be getting any design work. In fact, of course, everything has to be designed, even if it is designed badly with off-the-shelf solutions, so in reality you are likely to be getting something in between. Doesn't sound great, does it?

Controlling the cost

It is very difficult as a lay person to estimate how much a building project will cost. Yes, you can find rules of thumb in terms of cost per square metre, but domestic projects are notoriously variable. You will therefore be relying largely on your architect and, at a later stage, your builder to tell you how much things will cost.

Start by thinking about how much you can afford for the project, and try to work to an estimate that leaves you with about 10 to 20% of your budget in hand. Almost inevitably, there will be some things that don't go to plan, elements that prove to be more expensive than anticipated, or you may just want to go for a better quality of finish.

There is a difference between what you are budgeting and what you can afford. Or at least there is for some people. It may be that the amount in your budget is all that you have available, in which case stick to it. But if you have some additional funds, it is perfectly reasonable to decide that a more ambitious solution will give you more pleasure, and to go with that.

You need to talk to your architect very clearly about what you can afford, and do question costs. Many ambitious architects want to create the best building possible, so they may, from good motives, press you to go further. You need to be firm about this and to ask them to look at alternatives. You need to understand not only what the overall cost of your project will be, but also break it down into some of the larger elements.

The architect will have made an educated estimate of what the overall cost of the project will be, but it is not until you get bids from contractors that you will have a real cost to consider. Again, this is the moment when you need to do some hard thinking.

Make sure you have budgeted for everything. This does not just include the architect's fees and the builder's costs, but other costs that you may not have anticipated, such as planning approval and building regulations approval. There is also a Community Infrastructure Levy that local authorities can impose on new buildings, including significant extensions.[5] Don't forget about VAT either – not all prices are quoted with VAT.

There are a number of ways to approach these problems but there is one that is guaranteed not to work. That is discovering early on that the project is going to cost more than you can afford, but hoping that the issue will go away. It won't. There are a few projects that become cheaper over time but they are extremely rare.

6.11 WHEN MONEY IS TIGHT, YOU NEED TO BE CLEAR ABOUT YOUR PRIORITIES. THE CLIENT FOR THIS CAMBRIDGE HOUSE WAS PREPARED TO MAKE SACRIFICES ELSEWHERE IN ORDER TO STILL AFFORD A DOUGLAS FIR FLOOR. (SEE PAGE 92.)

Make sure the essentials are right

Plumbing and drains may not be glamorous, but make sure you think carefully about them and about the electrics before any more cosmetic works begin. You don't want to have to dig up that expensive floor at a later stage.

Some methods of construction, such as the use of cross-laminated timber (CLT) that is exposed internally, require a great deal of planning if you are not to see the services. Make sure you have enough power points and ventilation ducts at the beginning – putting them in later will be both expensive and unsightly. Making good is never as satisfying as getting it right first time.

Areas of uncertainty

With the best will in the world, there can be surprises in the course of construction, even if you are working with a highly professional team. Here are some to look out for:

Groundworks and excavation Once you start digging, you really don't know what you will uncover. A main sewer that was or wasn't on the survey? Poor ground conditions? You want to work with experts if you are building a basement, and want as good a survey as possible, but prepare for the unexpected.

Subsidence If you suspect there is subsidence, you will need to deal with it before doing any new work. It is notoriously hard to discover the extent and even the cause until work begins.

Damp Lift the floor to replace it and you may find a nasty surprise in the sub-floor, especially on the ground floor. Again, this needs dealing with.

Structural problems Old houses have typically undergone a lot of alteration, and not all of it will have been done well. Start looking behind the wall finishes and there may be some nasty surprises that need immediate action.

Electrical Some homes will prove to have distinctly antiquated electrical installations that do not meet modern standards and will need replacing. This is worth raising as a question at an early stage.

How to save money

If what you want is beyond your budget, or if unexpected extras make costs rise to beyond what you can afford, then you will need to find a way of spending less. There are various potential ways to manage your budget:

Can you spread the cost over a longer period? Could the flooring for the guest bedroom wait, if nobody is likely to stay in it for another year? Can you leave the space for the second oven in the kitchen until you can afford it? If you want to put in a lift to make life easier for you or a relative in later life, do you need it now, or could you just make room for it and install it later? Could the garden wait for a year or two?

Can you do without it? Be honest about your priorities. Some of us appreciate the finest wine, some drink the cheapest the supermarket has to offer and others have a taste that is somewhere in the middle. Decide how much you really care about the most gorgeous details. One client in this book was determined to have an expensive Douglas fir floor, but was happy to make savings elsewhere. Do you really need those beautiful door handles or that very expensive shower? Do the worktops have to be Corian? These are your decisions, and in some cases the answer to the questions will be 'yes', but the questions are certainly worth asking.

Can you minimise the risk? Contractors will often submit high bids if they are being asked to do something that is unfamiliar. They worry there may be hidden problems, and price accordingly. The architect may be able to deal with this by arranging for certain elements to be made elsewhere and putting them on a supply-only basis with the contractor. With the element of risk reduced, a contractor may be willing to drop their bid significantly.

Can you cheat? At least one project in this book saves money in the kitchen by putting custom-made doors onto off-the-shelf kitchen units. Can you use offcuts of materials in a creative way? Why not ask a decorator's merchant to mix the exact shade of paint that would be several times more expensive if you bought a proprietary product?

Can you stay put? For any project that involves a significant proportion of the home, it will be much easier for both the homeowner and the contractors if the property can be empty during construction. This, of course, means the owner will have to live elsewhere and, most probably, pay rent. If you can put up with the inconvenience, staying in your home amid the chaos may be a solution, and removes the worry that every extra day on the contract is costing you more money. Do discuss this early on with your architect and make your intention clear when appointing a contractor. One of the projects in this book was designed to have as few points of contact between the original and new building as possible, to accommodate a family that remained in residence. If you do choose to stay in your home, the construction process will almost certainly be longer, and may be more expensive, and it won't be fun. Perhaps you should consider that caravan in the garden after all.

Can you do it yourself? This is not for the faint-hearted, but some clients take on considerable responsibility for managing the project and/or carrying out some of the physical work themselves. If the latter, it is easiest if you are doing the finishing works, so the contractor can leave and hand over to you, rather than trying to negotiate a way of working alongside them.

When things go wrong

Everything that has been written above is aimed at ensuring that nothing should go wrong. But we know that disasters do happen. Have you ever watched an episode of Channel 4's *Grand Designs*? Even more seriously, things can go disastrously wrong. In November 2020, two houses in Chelsea collapsed during construction of a basement.

In May 2021, the BBC's *Rip Off Britain* show reported the case of a homeowner whose house collapsed when a builder working on an extension removed the roof without adequate precautions. It was going to cost £250,000 to put right, and the owner's insurer would not pay because it was the builder's responsibility. The builder's insurer would not pay because the builder had not provided full information.[6]

All you can really do about disasters like this is prevent them happening. Check the qualifications of everybody involved, and make sure the appropriate surveys have been done. You do not need an engineering degree to know that you should ask who has checked the work, and they should hold suitable qualifications. If something is worrying you, it is better to be a bit of nuisance than to end up as a rueful owner with a bill you cannot pay.

Fortunately, disasters like this are rare. What happens more frequently, although thankfully is still relatively uncommon, is that the client falls out with the architect or builder or both, or that one or other (more commonly the builder) goes out of business. Too often, in cases like this, the building is left unfinished.

The golden rule is never to pay for anything you have not had. Payments should be staged, and at the end of the project you should still be holding back a small amount of money for snagging – that is when the builder and architect come back and put right anything that has gone wrong. In this way, if the builder does let you down, it will be an annoyance and an inconvenience but the financial penalties should be as small as possible. It's not always easy, but you should be able to find somebody else to finish the work.

If you feel your architect has been negligent, and has not acted in accordance with their code of conduct, you can report them to the Architects Registration Board. In the most extreme case, they could be struck off and no longer allowed to call themselves an architect. This will not, however, bring you financial compensation. You would have to seek that through the courts, an expensive process and definitely a last resort. If you have a dispute, it is always best to look for ways of settling it.

Popping the champagne

Talking about what can go wrong is necessary, but hardly cheering. Remember that most projects largely go well, although there are likely to be minor niggles with a complex building (and every building is complex). The projects shown in the first section of this book show just how much can be achieved. In order to maximise your chances of success, you should:

- understand what you need

- choose your architect with care

- pay great attention to the briefing process

- discuss the architect's proposals and settle on a finished design

- agree any essential changes

- pay the bills.

If you do all this conscientiously, you should end up with a delightfully enhanced home. You may well echo the comments of some of the clients for the projects shown in this book:

'Considering the limited amount of "actual" floor space we have added, the feeling of space is incredible, and the amount of storage sets this project apart.'

'If we were ever in doubt about whether to engage the services of an architect in the redesign and extension of our family home, that was soon dispelled by the wonderful Gagarin Studio team.'

'Everything has been thought through – it's incredible.'

'We finally found an architect who can meet our brief for a super low-energy, low-carbon extension that works alongside the old house.'

'Much of the good design is summed up in the living room main window and box seat – economically enlarging an existing window space, and transforming it into one of the centrepieces of the building both visually and functionally.'

'It's lovely when sunny but what we didn't expect was how fun it would be in a storm.'

'The end result has just been fantastic. The best way to go forward with a project like this is to have an architect.'

It won't all be easy but at the end of the works it will be time to move back in or reinhabit the rest of your home. Get the kitchen equipment out of storage, put on the kettle and, ideally, throw a party. You will have completed one of the most daunting undertakings of your life and can celebrate the fact that your home is now far better than before, perhaps better even than you could have imagined.

Cheers!

directory

Architects featured in the case studies

Annabelle Tugby Architects
https://www.annabelletugbyarchitects.co.uk

Appleton Weiner
http://www.appletonweiner.co.uk

Arboreal Architecture
https://arborealarchitecture.com

Architecture for London
https://architectureforlondon.com

ArkleBoyce https://www.arkleboyce.co.uk

Bradley Van Der Straeten
https://b-vds.co.uk

CAN
https://can-site.co.uk

Cowper Griffith Architects
https://www.cowpergriffith.co.uk

David Connor Design
https://www.davidconnordesign.co.uk

Dominic McKenzie Architects
https://www.dominicmckenzie.co.uk

FAB Architects
https://www.fabarchitects.co.uk

Fraher & Findlay
https://fraherandfindlay.com

Gagarin Studio
https://www.gagarinstudio.co.uk

Groupwork
http://groupwork.uk.com

Hesketh Hayden
https://www.heskethhayden.co.uk

IF_DO
https://www.ifdo.co

Kate Darby Architects
https://www.katedarby.com

Knott Architects
https://knottarchitects.co.uk

Knox Bhavan Architects
https://knoxbhavan.co.uk

Liv Architects
https://www.livarchitects.co.uk

Lynch Architects
https://www.lyncharchitects.com

Napier Clarke Architects
http://napierclarke.co.uk

nimtim architects
https://www.nimtim.co.uk

O'Sullivan Skoufoglou Architects
https://www.osullivanskoufoglou.com

Paul Testa Architecture
https://paultestaarchitecture.co.uk

Poulsom Middlehurst
https://poulsommiddlehurst.com

Rider Stirland Architects
https://www.riderstirland.com

RX Architects
https://www.rxarchitects.com

Sam Tisdall Architects
http://www.samtisdall.co.uk

Scenario Architecture
https://scenarioarchitecture.com

Shape Architecture
https://www.shapearchitecture.co.uk

Studio 163
https://studio-163.com

Takero Shimazaki Architects
https://www.t-sa.co.uk

Transition by Design
https://transitionbydesign.org

Sources of information

https://arb.org.uk
Architects Registration Board; this is where to go in the unlikely case that you have a complaint.

https://find-an-architect.architecture.com
The RIBA's website for finding an architect; the best place to look.

https://www.architecture.com/digital-practice-tools/riba-contracts/riba-domestic-building-contract
The RIBA Domestic Building Contract.

https://nla.london/awards/dont-move-improve-2021
A source of interesting projects.

https://www.passivhaustrust.org.uk
Information on the Passivhaus approach to energy saving.

https://www.passivhaustrust.org.uk/competitions_and_campaigns/passivhaus-retrofit
EnerPHit is the version of Passivhaus that is suited to existing buildings and is likely to be more relevant to your project.

endnotes

Chapter 1

1   https://www.home.co.uk/guides/
    house_prices.htm?location=london
    (accessed December 2021).

2   https://www.tax.service.gov.uk/
    calculate-stamp-duty-land-tax/#/intro
    (accessed March 2022).

Chapter 2

1   https://www.statista.com/
    statistics/1190633/home-gym-
    equipment-sales (accessed March
    2022).

2   Burrows R, Graham S and Wilson
    A, 'Bunkering down? The geography
    of elite residential basement
    development in London', Urban
    Geography, 1 June 2021, https://www.
    tandfonline.com/doi/full/10.1080/027
    23638.2021.1934628 (accessed March
    2022).

3   https://www.themodernhouse.com/
    journal/contemporary-country-
    interiors-annabelle-tugby (accessed
    March 2022).

Chapter 4

1   https://www.renovategreen.co.uk/blog
    (accessed March 2022).

2   https://arborealarchitecture.com/
    projects/reuse-flat#:~:text=Reuse%20
    Flat%20is%20a%20
    project,sensory%20experience%20
    of%20the%20space (accessed March
    2022).

Chapter 6

1   https://www.architectsjournal.co.uk/
    aj100-data-and-profiles

2   https://historicengland.org.uk/listing/
    what-is-designation/listed-buildings
    (accessed March 2022).

3   https://www.planningportal.co.uk/
    permission/responsibilities/other-
    permissions-you-may-require/listed-
    buildings (accessed March 2022).

4   https://www.renovategreen.co.uk/blog
    (accessed March 2022).

5   https://www.gov.uk/guidance/
    community-infrastructure-levy
    (accessed March 2022).

6   https://www.bbc.co.uk/programmes/
    b00wck32 (accessed March 2022).

image credits

Page IV *CAN, photography by Jim Stephe*

Figure 0.1 *Scenario Architecture and David Rieser, photography by Matt Clayton*

Figure 1.1-5 *Bradley Van der Straeten*

Figure 1.6-9 *FAB Architects*

Figure 1.10-11, 1.13-14 *Liv Architects, photography by Matthew Smith Architectural Photography*

Figure 1.12 *Liv Architects*

Figure 1.15, 1.17-19 *Knott Architects, photography by Dome Photography*

Figure 1.16 *Knott Architects*

Figure 1.20-24 *Fraher & Findlay, photography by Jack Hobhouse*

Figure 1.25-28 *Gagarin Studio*

Figure 1.29 *Knox Bhavan Architects*

Figure 1.30-33 *Knox Bhavan Architects, photography by Nathalie Priem*

Figure 2.1 *Appleton Weiner, photography by Lyndon Douglas*

Figure 2.2-5 *Scenario Architecture and David Rieser, photography by Matt Clayton*

Figure 2.6 *Appleton Weiner*

Figure 2.7-10 *Appleton Weiner, photography by Lyndon Douglas*

Figure 2.11, 2.14-15 *Annabelle Tugby Architects*

Figure 2.12-13 *Clare Bingham*

Figure 2.16-20 *Groupwork, photography by Timothy Soar*

Figure 2.21-25 *RX Architects*

Figure 2.26-30 *Studio 163, photography by Emanuelis Photography*

Figure 3.1-5 *Poulsom Middlehurst, photography by Adam Scott Images*

Figure 3.6, 3.8-10 *IF_DO Architects, photography by Mariell Lind Hansen*

Figure 3.7 *IF_DO Architects*

Figure 3.11-15 *ArkleBoyce, photography by Nicholas Worley*

Figure 3.16-20 *Napier Clarke Architects*

Figure 3.21-25 *Takero Shimazaki Architects, photography by Anton Gorlenko*

Figure 3.26-30 *Arboreal Architecture, photography by Agnese Sanvito*

Figure 3.31-35 *Lynch Architects, photography by Taran Wilkhu*

Figure 4.1-5 *Sam Tisdall Architects, photography by Richard Chivers*

Figure 4.6, 4.9-10 *David Connor Design and Kate Darby Architects, photography by James Morris*

Figure 4.7-8 *David Connor Design and Kate Darby Architects*

Figure 4.11-15 *Dan Paton*

Figure 4.16, 4.18 *Hesketh Hayden*

Figure 4.17-20 *Francesco Russo / VIEW Pictures*

Figure 4.21-25 *Arboreal Architecture, photography by Agnese Sanvito*

Figure 4.26-30 *Cowper Griffith Architects, photography by Matthew Smith Architectural Photography*

Figure 5.1-2, 5.4-5 *Paul Testa Architecture, photography by Dug Wilders*

Figure 5.3 *Paul Testa Architecture*

Figure 5.6, 5.8-10 *Rider Stirland Architects, photography by Adam Scott*

Figure 5.7 *Rider Stirland Architects*

Figure 5.11, 5.13-15 *O'Sullivan Skoufoglou Architects, photography by Ståle Eriksen*

Figure 5.12 *O'Sullivan Skoufoglou Architects*

Figure 5.16-20 *Architecture For London*

Figure 5.21-24 *CAN, photography by Jim Stephenson*

Figure 5.25-27, 5.29 *Shape Architecture, photography by David Merewether*

Figure 5.28 *Shape Architecture*

Figure 5.30-34 *Dominic McKenzie, photography by Will Pryce*

Figure 5.35-36, 5.39 *nimtim architects, photography by Megan Taylor*

Figure 5.37-38 *nimtim architects*

Figure 6.1 *Lynch Architects, photography by Taran Wilkhu*

Figure 6.2 *Gagarin Studio*

Figure 6.3 *Groupwork, photography by Timothy Soar*

Figure 6.4 *Paul Testa Architecture, photography by Dug Wilders*

Figure 6.5 *Dominic McKenzie, photography by Will Pryce*

Figure 6.6 *Takero Shimazaki Architects, photography by Anton Gorlenko*

Figure 6.7 *Bradley Van der Straeten*

Figure 6.8 *Arboreal Architecture, photography by Agnese Sanvito*

Figure 6.9 *Shape Architecture*

Figure 6.10 *Scenario Architecture and David Rieser, photography by Matt Clayton*

Figure 6.11 *Sam Tisdall Architects, photography by Richard Chivers*

index

index